MANSTYLE

MANSTYLE

MANSTYLE

THE GQ GUIDE TO FASHION, FITNESS, AND GROOMING

BY PETER CARLSEN AND WILLIAM WILSON

Foreword by John Berendt

Clarkson N. Potter, Inc./Publishers NEW YORK

DISTRIBUTED BY CROWN PUBLISHERS, INC.

**For Arnold Gingrich,
founding editor, *Gentlemen's Quarterly*
(1903 – 1976)**

His guiding spirit lives on in
the people he inspired

Published simultaneously in Canada by General Publishing
Company Limited

First edition
Printed in the United States of America
Designed by Betty Binns

Library of Congress Cataloging in Publication Data

Carlsen, Peter.
    Manstyle: the GQ guide to fashion, fitness, and grooming.

    1. Men's clothing. 2. Fashion. 3. Grooming for
men. I. Wilson, William, 1948–   joint author.
TT618.C37   646'.32   77-9416
ISBN 0-517-53076-7
ISBN 0-517-53077-5 pbk.

Third Printing, June, 1978

Special thanks to Peter Maase for organizing our
impulses and to G.M., *saudade*.

PHOTOGRAPHERS' CREDITS

Arky & Barrett, pp. 14–17; Richard Ballarian, pp. 39, 41; Bill
Cahill, pp. 108–9, 112–13, 136, 140–42; André Carrara, p.
43; William Connors, p. 64 (bottom); Alberto Dell'Orto, p. 23
(left, top and bottom); Robert Farber, pp. 45–46; Fabrizio
Feri, p. 40; Raeanne Giovanni, pp. 100–101; Marco
Glaviano, pp. 23 (right, top), 47–57; Gary Gross, p. 26; Steve
Hiett, pp. 70, 71; Donald Kennedy, pp. 2, 4, 8, 9 (left), 11, 13,
34; Barry McKinley, pp. 122–23; Jacques Malignon, pp. 9
(right), 58; John Peden, pp. 6, 7, 29, 30; Denis Piel, pp. 10, 32,
38, 39 (right), 42; Leslie & George Priggen, pp. 60–61; Bob
Richardson, pp. 19, 20; Albert Rizzo, pp. 67, 73–91; Bob
Rossi, pp. 136–37; Alan Rowland (illustrations), pp. 132–33;
Albert Watson, pp. 12, 24, 25, 63, 68, 69, 102, 116, 118; Bruce
Weber, pp. 27, 126–29; Edwin Windmüller, p. 66.

Cover: Photographed by Barry McKinley. Clothes by Alex-
ander Julian, hat by Makins, attaché case by Mark Cross,
watch by Cartier. Cover design by Donald Sterzin.

CONTENTS

FOREWORD

The time finally came some years ago when I had eaten all the bad restaurant food I was going to eat and slept on one lumpy hotel bed too many, so in desperation I invented the Quality Tipoff. The Quality Tipoff is a kind of shortcut for people who want the best of everything—food, wine, lodgings, clothes, haircuts, cars, advice—but who don't have the time to research every last detail. The theory of the Quality Tipoff is that there is one clue, one minute, seemingly insignificant aspect of a thing, that informs you instantly about the whole.

For instance, when you are booking ahead for a hotel room you naturally want to find out about the comfort of the beds, the promptness of the room service, and the relative peace and quiet of the place. Using the Quality Tipoff you can ascertain all these things simply by asking, "Does your hotel deliver a complimentary morning newspaper to each room?" That's the Quality Tipoff for hotels. Don't ask me why, but it has never been known to fail; if the answer is yes, then it also follows that the beds are

firm, the service quick, and the atmosphere quiet.

Using the Quality Tipoff is the same as looking at the thickness of a carpenter's wood shavings to find out how skillfully he can make cabinets, or kicking the tires of a used car, or peering into a horse's mouth. Fine crystal goes *ping* rather than *clink* at the touch of a fingernail; that's almost all you have to know. A good suit or sports-jacket will have buttons made of bone rather than plastic, and if a custom-made suit is any good at all, the buttons on the sleeve will not be mere decoration but will actually button and unbutton.

There is also a Quality Tipoff for books on men's fashion and style, such as the one you are holding right now. In this case the key is formal wear. Find out how that subject is treated and you will know immediately whether to trust the book on anything else. If you are told that only the classic black-and-white uniform will do, you are in good hands. As it happens, I have read the chapter of this book on formal wear ("Going Formal"), and as a result I can vouch for the whole book. I myself, given the task, might have gone even further than the authors do on the subject of formal clothing. I might have warned that ruffled dress shirts are not only outré but intolerable and that pastel, brocaded, or otherwise patterned dinner jackets make the wearer look like an organ grinder's monkey. The authors of this book employ gentler turns of phrase, but nevertheless they set you straight. They explain the intricacies of formal and semiformal attire perfectly. Though elsewhere they also deal with the contemporary and the ephemeral, they do have a healthy respect for tradition.

Nor should that be surprising, when you consider the source. *Gentlemen's Quarterly* and its brother publication *Esquire* have been reasonably responsible reporters of taste and style for years, both magazines being descendants of the country's first magazine on men's style, *Apparel Arts*. The editors of *GQ*, who have written this book, have an eye for new trends but fortunately an acknowledged concern for established proprieties.

This book gives you sensible advice on building a wardrobe and tailoring it not only to your body but to your budget. It tells you about *details*—about pleated pants versus unpleated pants, for instance—about cuffs versus no cuffs, about how shirts are made and how to make sure they fit you.

This book certainly must be the first guide on style that has had anything to say about blue jeans. But if it is true that Fiorucci-designed jeans are selling for five hundred dollars a pair in Brazil, as the authors say, then the time for jeans has certainly come. And if you had any doubts about how to predict how much a pair of jeans will shrink when washed, you will learn here. You can also find out how to bleach jeans without ruining them. Lastly, in case you didn't know already, the authors tell you the derivations of the words *denim*, *jeans*, and *dungarees*. I am not ashamed to say I did not know and that I am delighted I do now.

If the authors seem a bit bearish about fashion, it is only fashion in the commercial sense and in the sense of the whimsical dictates of self-appointed style setters, two aspects of fashion worthy of disdain. Whether a thing is in or out of fashion really doesn't matter after all, and it certainly doesn't matter whether the manufacturers are pushing or not. The bottom line is taste. For, in fact, we live in an era dominated by very bad taste, particularly in respect to clothing. Turn your back for an instant and another poor unfortunate has paid good money for a leisure suit and a dozen others have outfitted themselves in doubleknits, head to toe. There are just so many pitfalls, so much gaucherie, so many offenses to the eye everywhere you look that what you really want in a book about style for men is an intelligent regard for enduring good taste. And this is what you have here.

Furthermore, this book tells you all you need to know about fabrics, and it even tells you the best way to pack a suitcase. It gives you hints on how to care for your clothes once you've got them. And for good measure the authors append chapters on proper eating, grooming, and keeping in shape.

There are only two pieces of advice I would add to the plethora of pointers offered here. The first is the observation by Oscar Wilde that "a well-tied tie is the first serious step in life." It does not matter that this is an age of the open collar; the import of Wilde's dictum is still undimished: it is fine to be casual, but it helps to have a grasp of fundamentals. The second is to draw your attention to something Fred Astaire once said: "I often take a brand-new suit or hat and throw it up against the wall a few times to get that stiff, square newness out of it." Once you have refined your act to that degree, you're home free.

JOHN BERENDT

INTRODUCTION

DRESSING WELL IS THE BEST REVENGE

Fashion has always been one of civilization's hardier flowers. Whether the economy waxes or wanes, whether the times are good or bad, style has gone on tirelessly evolving and changing and even repeating itself. Recently, however, as we closed the door on the prosperity of the sixties and began to face the realities of a new age with very different priorities (such as how to get from point A to point B with a minimum of disruption to the national economy), certain questions have arisen about the future of dressing well. Although we all know that it's the best revenge, the question has become how to achieve maximum effect for minimum effort in these confusing times. In short, what guidelines *are* there for the new era?

Predicting the future is, of course, a notoriously elusive sport, and in terms of fashion it can be a veritable trap as well. In today's restless world the projection of a style into the next decade or even into the next season is as controversial as the question of taste. Nevertheless, style is the essence of fashion, and it keys the mood of an era as much as old movies and photographs do. In the seventies, the gathering impact of a dozen movements in the arts, politics, and pop psychology has contributed to the beginnings of a mosaic of culture rather than a single dominant aesthetic. Consequently, style has divided itself into many different splinter groups. Fashion today consists of multiple choices; in the future it may become totally eclectic.

Nonetheless, there are still attitudes, ways of looking at dress, that strike certain responsive chords in society. Clothes are often a witty commentary on life and fashion and any man interested in dressing well is sure to be one who enjoys what might still be termed a sophisticated way of life. He knows that, as with all subtleties, there are standards to be observed and rules that are still capable of holding vestigial authority, however flouted they may be. It is also obvious that many rules exist not only because taste and style are being upheld but also because doing something correctly is usually the most functional, to say nothing of being the easiest, way.

The first impulse, then, is to turn (as we are all wont to do in times of perplexity) to the rule books. The trouble is that all those discreet, conventional little manuals that used to deal with everyone's anxious questions about etiquette as well as fashion do's and don'ts have long been out of print. Hardy survivors on library shelves are apt to yield such cheerful gems as "give yourself a lift by wearing different-colored accessories with your basic gray suit." Obviously, whatever direction we're going, it isn't going to be backward. Hence *Manstyle*. We feel it's about time that a new set of guidelines appeared, based on current realities, taking into account the complexity and contrariness of a society that in so many ways is changing faster than ever before.

One of the better side effects of our current situation could well be the growing realization that fashion is now rooted in reality. Nostalgia is a dead end, with nothing to offer a man who wishes to look good and function well in our world. That's why *Manstyle* is devoted to clothes that speak a modern language and that deal in an unsentimental and clear-eyed way with the problems of fashion, fitness, and grooming for men *today*.

MANSTYLE

Emily Post said it all when it comes to men's business wear: "Whatever the fashion of the moment, if a man's suit fits him well, is appropriate to whatever he may be doing, and is not overly conspicuous in style or color, he may rest assured that he will be labeled well-dressed in any community."

Here, proof of Miss Post's theory. Our executive friend wears *the* classic two-button, single-breasted business suit, with a straight-collar shirt, geometric-motif tie, and solid-color pocket handkerchief. Not an element is out of place, gratuitous, or attention seeking. The total effect is neither intimidating nor easily forgotten. In addition, it inspires confidence and trust.

CHAPTER 1
BUSINESS WEAR

As far as we can tell, the question the shrewd businessman asks himself—or should ask himself—more than any other is not, "How can I make more money?" That approach to success he recognizes for what it is: a matter of sheer animal appetite, not exactly beside the point, perhaps, but not deserving of his full intellectual scrutiny, either. No, the question this man turns over and over in his mind is more likely to be, "How can I express myself more fully? How can I capitalize on who I am, drawing on those qualities and abilities that are uniquely mine—without alienating every-body within a hundred-yard radius, with-out seeming like either an insufferable egotist or a hopeless amateur?" Here we see the sacrifice business has traditionally exacted of its practitioners, the diluting, even disguising, of one's individuality so that one will be found acceptable by one's boss, colleagues, and clients, separately and simultaneously.

One *does*, unless one is president of one's own corporation (and even then there's the public image to worry about), have to tone oneself down considerably to do business. Idiosyncrasy and flair, though they may be the secret ingredients that make any number of partnerships, mergers, and deals really work, cannot always be given actual expression in any but the loosest pro-fessional settings. And even there you'll find precedents, codes, and policies that curtail the nature and degree of what seems to be unlimited freedom. Once again, it's not a simple matter of what's traditional on the one hand or extremist on the other, but simply of what's accepted within the established boundaries of your profession, corporation, and, finally, your own office. You have to understand what the rules are and demonstrate your ability to play by them—skillfully, impeccably—before you can twist them a bit to suit you and your own sense of appropriateness and purpose.

We don't have to tell you that in the boardroom even more than in the ballroom or on the links (as men's fashion pages used to put it) nothing stands to confirm your essence—or reveal it—as immediately and

Business suits should convey a feeling of dignity and substance, but they don't have to be drab. Here are two that, as much by dint of their color as anything else, provide less prosaic alternatives. *Far left,* a polyester-and-wool three-piece suit. Note the slightly curved lapel and the fullness of the trousers, both indicative of the European approach to tailoring. Most telltale, however, is the visible highness of the armholes, that point where sleeve meets jacket. Although the resultant tightness inhibits freedom of movement somewhat, it also confers a degree of stylization that can be helpful to a man interested in cultivating an image of sophistication.

Left, a much more typically American approach to style and fit. Again a three-piece suit, this time of polyester, wool, and mohair, but this time there's an amplitude that European tailoring seldom suggests. Note, too, the collar pin, which can single-handedly make an outfit soar, especially in conjunction with a silk pocket handkerchief.

irreversibly as what you're wearing. Whether this is a holdover from medieval guild days, when professional men really did dress in uniforms that served to identify to an illiterate public their talents and intentions, or whether this dates from America's own make-it-or-break-it nineteenth century, notorious for the opportunities it afforded upstarts and nouveaux riches to legitimize themselves through shameless aping of the manners and dress of the Establishment, or whether it simply represents a working out of modern, essentially class-bound reactions to certain icons as elemental and seemingly innocent as trench coats and vests whereby (depending on the circumstances of one's birth) one trusts or refuses to trust the man in the black hat—it's hard to say. The fact remains that, though you are of course a person of considerable complexity, you're going to be read by colleagues and clients alike as if you were the *Daily News.* That's not to say that they'll grasp your true essence, only—and this is infinitely more dangerous—that they'll *think* they have.

Now we're not arguing that one should sacrifice wit, imagination, and high style to the inherent cautiousness of the corporate life, only that this is no time to be either oblivious, taking unnecessary risks simply because you haven't thought to analyze your work situation, or self-conscious, paralyzed by an overrefined elegance or formality that's not in keeping with the way your profession does things. Everybody knows that, if he's chosen banking as a career, he's at the same time chosen a life of essential conservatism. His suits no less than his handshake are expected to reflect the fact that he's trustworthy, level-headed, and in control. That means dark suits of a traditional (i.e., reassuring and authoritarian) cut, vests, white shirts, and no beards or bow ties.

What people don't realize is that there are rules just as binding for the dress of those in the so-called creative professions. Architects, advertising copywriters, music-company executives are under as much

pressure to project *their* sense of youth, energy, and overall brashness as bankers are of conservatism. It's incumbent on them to fit in with their corporate roles, too, roles that are, if anything, harder to define and crystallize. Once defined, though, they must be honored. An architect who shows up in his office one morning in a three-piece chalk-stripe suit with a watch chain and collar pin glinting magisterially would be as jarring to his colleagues' and clients' sense of propriety as the banker who greets his loan holders in a velour jumpsuit. Propriety, it seems clear, is a matter not so much of formality as of suitability, appropriateness, and consistency. Couple propriety with force and a soupçon of imagination and you've got the makings of a successful businessman—and a successful businessman's wardrobe.

Here, three variations on a highly civilized theme, the double-breasted business suit in dark gray wool. *Far left*, the basic solid. *Above*, a pin stripe. *Below*, a chalk stripe—more muted, more widely spaced than the pin.

A note about double-breasteds in general. First, they're tricky. They go in and out of style faster than almost any other men's wear item and, consequently, they have limited investment value. If you want to be able to wear your suits three or more years from now, you will be much safer with the single-breasted model. Second, if you're heavy, or even a little thick, don't wear one. Double-breasteds require a trim body and above-average height to be carried off with optimal élan. But, on the proper frame and correctly accessorized, they'll confer more in the way of bearing and breeding than you ever dreamed possible.

More heat-of-the-day suggestions. *Far left,* a double-breasted Dacron-and-wool number. In addition to his suit, the man here is doing two other things right. His briefcase is the kind that suggests its owner wields at least some power: it's big, it's burnished, and it has gold edges and corners. And his glasses, with simple but solid frames, lend an air of authority to his stance and, in fact, make him seem older and more assured than he may be in reality.

Left, not to be outdone, is a man wearing a peak-edged polyester-and-wool suit, looking at his exceedingly expensive Rolex watch. Power is, we have to conclude, where you find it.

Below, a sport coat, double-breasted vest, and trousers combination that, while at home in only a limited number of business environments, is to our minds a successful stab at elegance, coupled with a sense of humor and self-confidence. (The bicycle, which presumably won't be ridden in the office, helps a great deal, of course.) Note how the boldly striped tie provides ironic commentary on the essential sobriety of the jacket and double-breasted vest.

Valentino, the well-known Italian couturier, designed what may be the last word in the traditional three-piece suit. Here, a solid black wool jacket, vest, and pants. The ensemble, made of the finest fabrics available, typifies the European—and specifically the Roman—rethinking of basic English tailoring and is very, very expensive. (This three-piece combination costs roughly $600.) Now, the point is this: there are some business situations in which this kind of extravagant dressing will impress, and probably render speechless, the men you're dealing with, the men you're attempting to sell yourself to. But on the other hand, it may prove too much, provoking hostility and perhaps contempt. Even corporate presidents, unless they're known for their fashionability or are working in very glamorous industries indeed, think twice before cultivating such self-conscious elegance. These are perfect suits—so perfect that they're better off saved for occasions where you won't be found guilty of deliberate ostentation.

On this page and the next two are illustrations of what we suggested earlier: that there are some offices, in fact whole professions, where suits are simply out of place. Look here, for a case in point. What could look more natural stepping down from that platform in an ultramodern design firm than a bold-colored glazed cotton blazer with khaki pants and a plaid vest? Or below, at the drafting table, a milk-chocolate leather jacket that bears out the form-should-follow-function adage, the principle on which all good design rests. Why get dressed up, why wear a tie, why for that matter expect your colleague to be skirted and pearled when what will obviously sell blueprints is a personal —as well as environmental—ambience of controlled informality?

This page features the sports jacket, a compromise between the traditionalism of the suit and the renegade informality of the safari jacket. The sports jacket is now as acceptable as the suit in some professions and, frankly, is more appropriate in those where the deals are being made in an atmosphere of enforced casualness. Authoritative but not stuffy, easy but not overly loose, the sports jacket, when properly coordinated with pants and, as in these two shots, a vest, can be mightily convincing. *At left*, a three-piece outfit that unabashedly advocates pattern-on-pattern; in this case a large check (the jacket), a smaller check (the vest), and a pair of pleated wool pants. Note how the solid-colored but highly textured tie helps pull it all together. *Below*, the converse: two solids of different intensity and a discreet check manage to convey a single impression: competence. Again, the tie and shirt, though strong enough, aren't themselves vying for attention: a good idea when one's adapting to business use what used to be thought of as sports clothes.

In the movie industry it's an unwritten law that the excess winds up on the cutting-room floor. That means that though you can experiment, even innovate, you can't overdo. If one's going to bend the rules to suit oneself, one had better do so impeccably. *Left*, a lightweight safari jacket with a wool sweater and cream-colored linen trousers. *Below*, a shirt-jacket worn with a simple white shirt and scarf. Note that both men have avoided patterns, too-bright colors, anything that threatens to distract or that smacks of unprofessionalism—except, perhaps, for those sunglasses. But what can you do with a movie star?

Before we let you go—in effect, before we let you leave the office—we do want to talk about what may be the most stringent of all business situations: the job interview. The pressures inherent in this often barbaric procedure may be no greater than those you'll face every day—assuming you get the job—but they're considerably more difficult to beat. That's because, in the space of an hour or less, you've really got to do it all: you've got to prove not only your desirability but also suggest your ultimate worth. It's a lot like being a slide under a microscope. The amount of merciless scrutiny (or equally merciless apathy) that's being directed at you is enormous. And you've got but a single opportunity to catch this version of a scientist's eye—and hold it.

So don't let what you're wearing to an interview ruin your chances of getting the job you want. You don't necessarily want to strive for total blandness, but you do need to be very careful. Here, then, are some practical—and highly specific—profession-by-profession caveats, compiled by John Berendt at *Esquire*. Don't show up in another crowded (or terrifyingly empty) corporate reception area without having noted them.

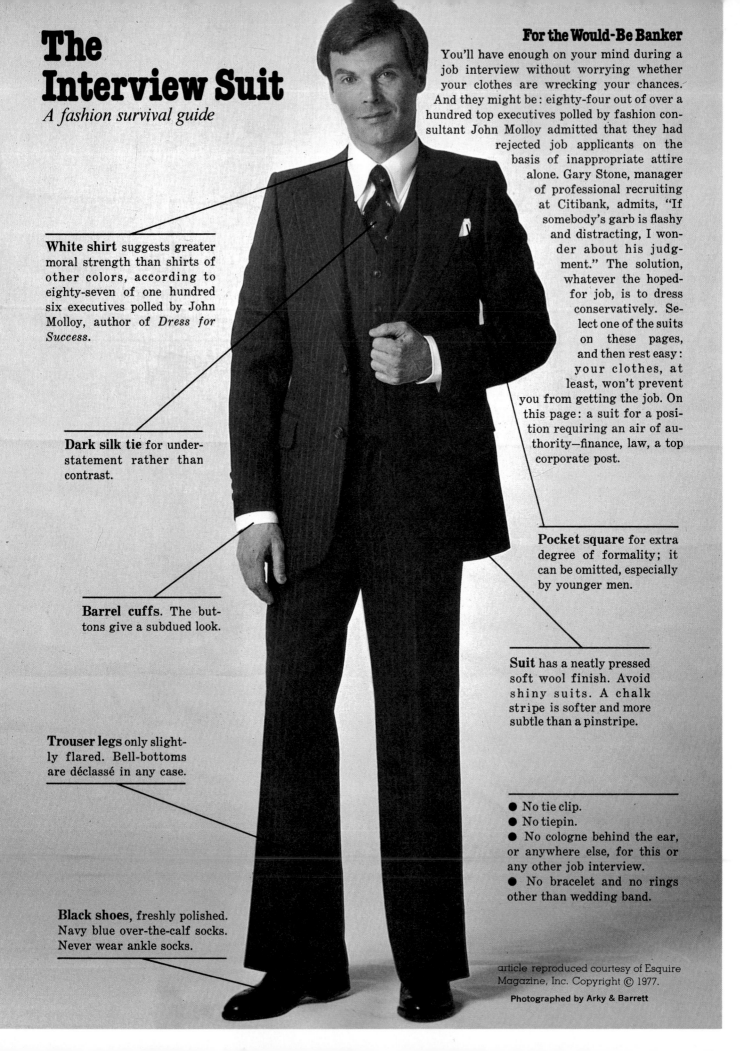

The Interview Suit

A fashion survival guide

For the Would-Be Banker

You'll have enough on your mind during a job interview without worrying whether your clothes are wrecking your chances. And they might be: eighty-four out of over a hundred top executives polled by fashion consultant John Molloy admitted that they had rejected job applicants on the basis of inappropriate attire alone. Gary Stone, manager of professional recruiting at Citibank, admits, "If somebody's garb is flashy and distracting, I wonder about his judgment." The solution, whatever the hoped-for job, is to dress conservatively. Select one of the suits on these pages, and then rest easy: your clothes, at least, won't prevent you from getting the job. On this page: a suit for a position requiring an air of authority—finance, law, a top corporate post.

White shirt suggests greater moral strength than shirts of other colors, according to eighty-seven of one hundred six executives polled by John Molloy, author of *Dress for Success*.

Dark silk tie for understatement rather than contrast.

Barrel cuffs. The buttons give a subdued look.

Trouser legs only slightly flared. Bell-bottoms are déclassé in any case.

Black shoes, freshly polished. Navy blue over-the-calf socks. Never wear ankle socks.

Pocket square for extra degree of formality; it can be omitted, especially by younger men.

Suit has a neatly pressed soft wool finish. Avoid shiny suits. A chalk stripe is softer and more subtle than a pinstripe.

● No tie clip.
● No tiepin.
● No cologne behind the ear, or anywhere else, for this or any other job interview.
● No bracelet and no rings other than wedding band.

article reproduced courtesy of Esquire Magazine, Inc. Copyright © 1977.

Photographed by Arky & Barrett

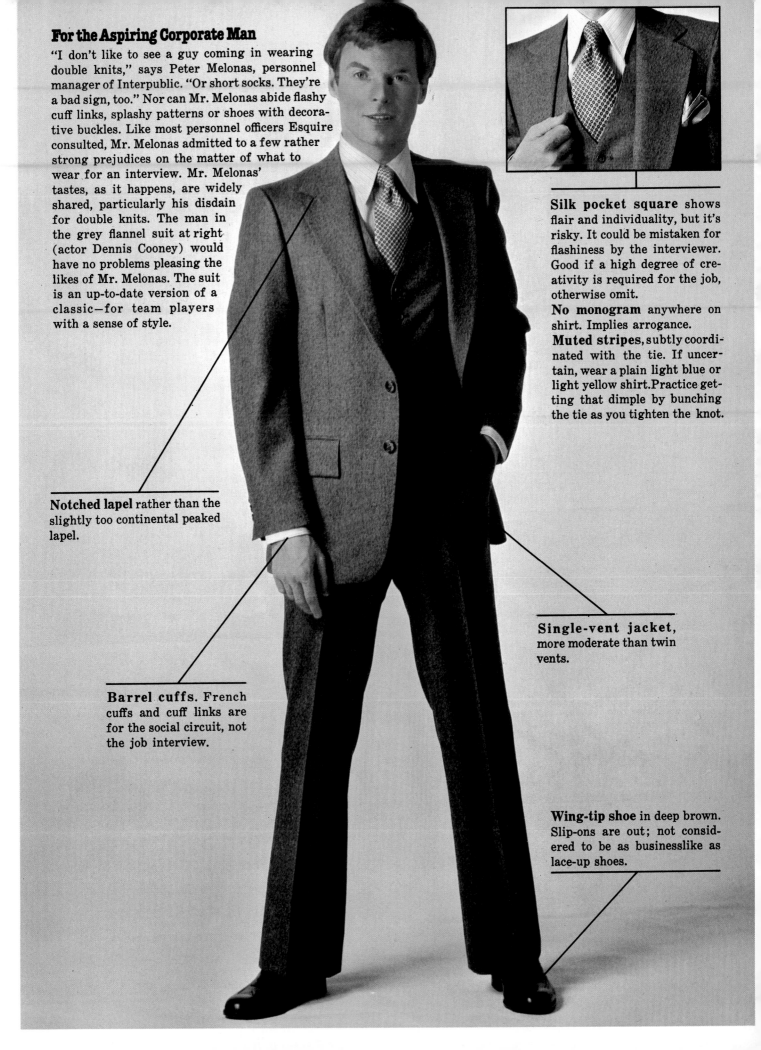

For the Aspiring Corporate Man

"I don't like to see a guy coming in wearing double knits," says Peter Melonas, personnel manager of Interpublic. "Or short socks. They're a bad sign, too." Nor can Mr. Melonas abide flashy cuff links, splashy patterns or shoes with decorative buckles. Like most personnel officers Esquire consulted, Mr. Melonas admitted to a few rather strong prejudices on the matter of what to wear for an interview. Mr. Melonas' tastes, as it happens, are widely shared, particularly his disdain for double knits. The man in the grey flannel suit at right (actor Dennis Cooney) would have no problems pleasing the likes of Mr. Melonas. The suit is an up-to-date version of a classic—for team players with a sense of style.

Silk pocket square shows flair and individuality, but it's risky. It could be mistaken for flashiness by the interviewer. Good if a high degree of creativity is required for the job, otherwise omit.

No monogram anywhere on shirt. Implies arrogance.

Muted stripes, subtly coordinated with the tie. If uncertain, wear a plain light blue or light yellow shirt. Practice getting that dimple by bunching the tie as you tighten the knot.

Notched lapel rather than the slightly too continental peaked lapel.

Barrel cuffs. French cuffs and cuff links are for the social circuit, not the job interview.

Single-vent jacket, more moderate than twin vents.

Wing-tip shoe in deep brown. Slip-ons are out; not considered to be as businesslike as lace-up shoes.

For the Prospective Salesman

"In sales and marketing you call on a wide range of people, many of whom might be put off by extremes," says John Macomber, Inter-continental Hotels' marketing chief. "So, it's safest to wear suits of moderate design," he says, "as opposed to, say, an Italian cut with sharp, tailored shoulders and tapered waist." Mr. Macomber recalls one unsuccessful interviewee who was more than qualified for a marketing job, except that he wore a pinkish double-knit suit and purple patent-leather shoes. He'd have been far better off if he'd worn something on the order of this salt-and-pepper tweed suit. It's casually dressy, not as austere as a dark blue or dark grey suit and more outgoing and friendly.

Bright regimental tie in complementary but traditional colors is outgoing and commands attention.

Pocket square in solid color or none at all.

Solid-color broadcloth shirt is a must with busy fabric.

Fingernails trimmed.

Suit jacket is always unbuttoned when you sit down.

Vest plus classic cut keeps the suit conservative in spite of bright fabric.

Cordovan shoes have a richness in color and finish. Match with belt.

For the Account-Exec Hopeful

"At an interview, a man should dress for the part he expects to play," says Anne Wright, vice-president and personnel manager of the advertising giant J. Walter Thompson. "For an art director, that could be a turtleneck. For a prospective account executive, it means a suit. Of course, once he has been hired and finds out, for instance, that on Fridays (when there are no client meetings) everyone wears sports jackets in the office, fine. Certainly, it goes without saying that we expect to see clean finger-nails and a clean-cut overall look." The part played by an executive in advertising is that of an energetic, informed man of the world; not too fastidious; relaxed. An ideal costume for such a role (or for any number of other jobs—TV, teaching, public relations) would be the muted plaid suit worn here. Be sure to leave topcoat, rubbers and packages in the waiting room; never bring them into the interview with you: too much clutter.

A change of tie (a silk foulard instead of a stripe) for a quieter look. Soft blue oxford-cloth button-down shirt for a casual accent. A white shirt would kill the outfit.

Silk pocket square optional. If you wear it, don't fiddle with it during interview.

Belt in a blending rather than contrasting color. No big flashy buckles.

Plaid pattern indicates independence of spirit. For interview, choose a quiet plaid. Red stripe introduces a warm note.

Grained wing-tip shoe: tweedy.

CHAPTER 2
YOUR PRIVATE LIFE

Perhaps you're wondering what exactly makes us think we have the right to voice an opinion on the subject of how you put yourself together on your days off, when neither the restrictions of the office nor the conventions of the occasional formal ceremony apply. Maybe you consider this to be meddling of the worst—and silliest—kind.

Before you skip over this chapter, convinced either that you know it all or that there's simply nothing to know, let us get a word or two in. "Private life" isn't really all that private; there *are* others involved. Friends and neighbors, to begin with, are in a position to watch what you're doing, to observe the choices you make in this area, as in all others—and to pass judgment accordingly. Even on your days off, you have an image and an identity to maintain.

Then, too, there's the question of the woman or women there may be in your life. She is likely to have a strong sense of who you are and how you should dress while you're being that person. Of course, it's up to you whether to confirm her views or vigorously combat them, though we think it's

reasonable to assume that you've chosen to spend your time with her at least in part on the basis of how she interprets you. Whatever. The point is, you've got an audience there that's interested, appreciative, and (best of all) prepared to help. We realize this is no decade for glib generalizations on the subject of women, but we can't help noticing that a lot of the ones we know are awfully good shoppers and have an instinctive understanding of such basic fashion concepts as color, texture, and fit. If you have a hard time in front of that three-way tailor's mirror, it might not be a bad idea to have another pair of eyes along. And her eyes will probably take in more than those of your drinking buddy, accountant, or cousin from Sewickley.

Most of all, there's yourself to think about. Those same three concepts—color, texture, and fit—can be sources of tremendous satisfaction *if* you've taken the trouble to deal with them correctly. They are also great inducers of sensuality, both in you the wearer and in her the onlooker. Why willingly sacrifice a chance to make an

SATURDAY NIGHTS

The telephone rings—and you get the message. It's going to be a night on the town. You'll want to look your best, yet appear almost negligent with regard to the degree of attention you seem to have paid to yourself. In short: throwaway chic. How will you pull it off? You'll need guts, respect for glamor and, most importantly, a fine eye for nuance. It's often the subtle extra that you add—or omit—at the last minute that winds up casting the spell.

When cocktails run into dinner and dinner runs into dancing till dawn, wrap things up loosely. *Below left,* sweater over sweater— over— that's right—sweater, with cotton duck trousers. *Right,* a similar matching of wool sweater and trousers of the same material and color. The effect is subtle, inviting attention and commendation, yet it shuns cheap publicity. Coordination even more than contrast can make stringent demands on your resources, your sense of color, fabric, and level of fashion diction.

When the evening promises to involve a high degree of social contact, be it of an easy double-date variety or the crush of a major gallery opening, let understatement be your guiding principle. Allow unusual fabrics, ones that are lightweight and hang naturally on the body, that won't wrinkle, and that feel good next to your skin to carry the day. Simple color schemes count, too, by refusing to add to the congestion and competition in a room already full—possibly too full—of people. *At left,* a lamb suede shirt makes for a simple silhouette, without sacrificing either sensuality or individuality. A pair of Dacron-and-wool slacks promises to retard wrinkling. The only nonessential included is a white silk scarf, which adds a feeling of modest elegance to this man's look.

Below: Wear a tie when dining out if you want, but alter your personal bill of fare by putting on a cardigan sweater instead of the expected sportcoat. Sometimes people—especially people at their leisure, with time to observe and react, as is the case with restaurant-goers—like to be taken up just a bit short. And this is one way to do it without sacrificing your legitimacy.

Here, the perfect dressy over-coat, a velvet-collared chesterfield in shades of gray and green. It's possible that you'll want to reserve it for special occasions and wear something, well, easier—like a Burberry's trenchcoat with button-in lining—on most days.

impression that's simultaneously powerful *and* seductive—and that honors the strictures of your own personal aesthetic?

In short, there's a lot to think about and to be alert to in dressing for one's private life. The guidelines are really fairly simple and have more to do with logic than with law. Here are some now:

□ Call as much attention to yourself as you can, but never more than the most-to-be-envied man in the room is calling to himself. And never more than you can hold up under for the duration of the event, whether it's an hour of cocktails or a weekend of being a house guest.

□ Let your image be as specific as you can make it without confining yourself unduly. Punk, aristocrat, scholar, jock—they're all fine identities, if you can carry them off, if you can persuade by your manner and your choice of words that they're something you have a legitimate claim (not necessarily by birth, or even build) to. Having a specific image gives those around you a feeling that they can categorize you, that they know who you are. They may be wrong, of course, but just the existence of that feeling on their part furthers interpersonal commerce, and that's what it's really all about.

□ When in doubt as to whether to do the elegant (or formal or outrageous or generally hyper) thing, don't. It's much better to be the person who's dressed down than the one who's obviously made too much of an effort and is as a result bent double under the weight of his own cumbersome armor. Better to save your grand gestures for nights when there's a feeling of excessiveness in the air, when it's clear that a double-breasted white silk suit—or a pair of thrift-shop lederhosen—is exactly what's called for, what's going to win you raves. You'll recognize such a night as you see it approaching, and so will those you're going to be spending it with.

□ Remember that you're going to be evaluated on a number of scales, the most important single one of which has tradition at one end of it and innovation at the other. This is an opposition that many, many people react strongly to. (It's what's given us conservative and liberal politicians, orthodox and reform religious leaders, classical and acid-rock radio stations.) You can't afford to ignore it. Take into account your own nature, the nature of the occasion at hand, and whether you want to blend into it or try to turn it around. We won't tell you not to wear those lederhosen—with, for that matter, a pair of Cork-Ease—to a barbecue in Scarsdale, but be prepared to be considered nothing short of shocking if you do. Likewise, a madras jacket at a Rolling Stones concert isn't, strictly speaking, incorrect, but it isn't going to make you one with your stadium mates, either. In general it's best not to set out to abrade the sensibilities of the others who are likely to be present at barbecue or concert unless, of course, that's part of your game plan.

In this chapter we try to show you some of your primary options, a sampling of what sorts of things are available for wear in a wide variety of situations: on country weekends, on the tennis court, for upbeat Saturday nights (yes, the tradition still persists and will for as long as there are Monday mornings forcing one to have a good time on schedule), and back in your own living room.

Top right, an écru-colored V-neck sweater of Italian extraction, in the so-called popcorn stitch, worn over a turtleneck and fortified by a wool serape over one shoulder. The serape is unfurled below. Perfect for an early November hike—or a mid-April siesta. Note the contrast it furnishes to the simple string cotton pullover with an asymmetrical neck at the far right. This is strictly hot-weather wear—and yet, to our way of thinking, at least, it's as representative of the sweater sensibility as is anything made of wool.

THE ALL-PURPOSE SWEATER

Of all the elements that go to make up the wardrobe that you'll be dipping into for those afternoons of shopping, crisp mornings in the country, and sultry evenings in distant island paradises, none is more critical or more basic than the sweater. Of course, it can be the most traditional accessory and lender of simple warmth going: witness the shetland crew necks we all grew up with and that many of us think are worth keeping in stock. But sweaters can also scale the battlements of fashion innovation and high style, and they can function as effectively in summer as in winter.

Take a cable-knit ride and add another scenic loop to your wardrobe. The sweater-vest helps soften the mood and assures that, if you wish, you can still stride into the office (certain offices, anyway) on your day off.

Here, in the big picture, tweed, suede, and corduroy comprise a triple alliance; in fact, they were sold in this same combination, last fall, right off the rack. No problems here, we grant you. But their strength becomes even more evident when they're split up and allowed to take off individually, in the looks you put together to suit your own needs.

Try dropping the vest in favor of a sweater. Then loosen up the look by climbing into a pair of jeans.

MULTIPLE CHOICES

In your time "off-camera" there is infinitely more potential for genuine creativity than in your time on. For one thing, you don't have colleagues and clients expecting you to reinforce their possibly parochial image of you. For another, there is simply more time and energy available to you to get dressed for a football game or a gallery opening than there is at 7:30 every morning when that alarm goes off. But perhaps most important, both clothing manufacturers and retailers are finely attuned to your needs in this area and have provided you with all you'll ever need by way of raw materials to make your own individual look. Here, fashion has truly come alive in the last twenty years or so.

When is a sportcoat not a sportcoat? When it's a blouson jacket. Just leave the basic outfit untouched, combining the blouson's essential informality with the dressiness of the shirt-and-tie underpinnings. You see, you've created a whole new look.

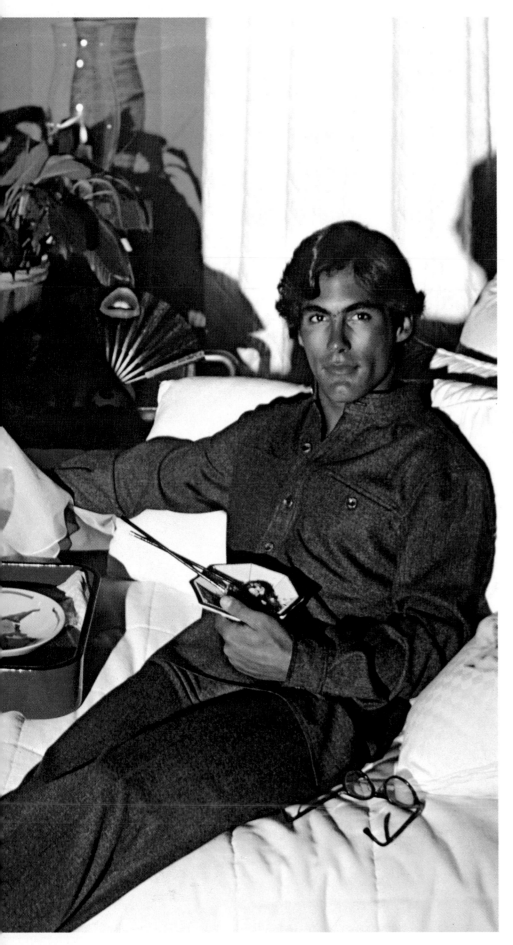

Private life has, at its best, a distinctly physical dimension to it. This can manifest itself in the pool, on the tennis court, in fact on playing fields of all descriptions. The point is, you're playing hard—in many cases, as hard as you'd ever dream of working. But it shouldn't cause wardrobe problems for you. To the contrary, dressing for sport is almost easier than any other kind of dressing. Simply choose clothes that are loose and cool, giving your body every opportunity to perform well, and honor such conventions concerning color, long pants versus shorts, and so on as exist in the sport and at the playing facility in question. Most of all, remain level-headed, relegating fantasy and extravagance to the moments *after* the game, the time that's defined by the *après* in *après-ski.*

The man at right returns a volley wearing that most traditional of garments, the cable-stitched tennis sweater. His light yellow shorts match the bit of yellow at the sleeve and neck of the sweater. It's all so straightforward and simple. Visit a good sporting goods store and you'll see what we mean.

When it comes to lounge wear there's not a lot to say. The central concept is not, as you may have suspected from the use of the word *lounge,* comfort. It's seductiveness, really—the talent to get other people to do what you want them to do and quite possibly what they had no intention of doing when you opened the door and let them in.

Gray flannel, long considered the last gasp of conservatism, proves that it's as much at home over impromptu Chinese food in the bedroom as over annual reports in the boardroom. Here, a wool and nylon top and trousers combination, structured in that a tailor's hand is evident, yet absolutely unconfining.

JEANEOLOGY

A FITTING TRIBUTE TO AMERICA'S MOST ENDURING FASHION INNOVATION

Chances are that of all the items you incorporate into your private-life wardrobe, none is going to serve you better, longer, or more loyally than your blue jeans. In an era of flashes-in-the-pan, gimmickry, and shoddy construction methods they stand out dramatically as one of the smartest long-term investments you can make. Taboo in the fifties, first teen-treasured and later demonstration-proved in the sixties, jeans have become fashion's common denominator in the seventies. The very word is synonymous with comfort, versatility, and contemporaneity.

FOREIGN INTRIGUE

Stories have been circulating for years concerning the lofty prices American jeans, especially Levi's (in particular used Levi's) fetch on the Soviet Union's black market. Reports vary. In 1974, an $8 pair of new jeans was said be able to command $90. It's estimated that the price of a pair of new jeans today is creeping toward $150.

In Brazil the most sought-after status item this year is the straight-legged, blue-denim jeans made by Fiorucci, the Italian retail chain. Availability: virtually nil; price: $500. A São Paulo boutique managed to stock a dozen pairs, but they were gone in a matter of days, each at that $500 price. This state of affairs derives in part from Brazil's 300-percent import duty and partly from the fact that Fiorucci is virtually unknown in South America and hence has tremendous cachet.

FADE OUT

So you've bought a new pair of jeans, gotten exactly the style you want in the size you need, and still you're unhappy. Of course; who wants to invest a year of his life breaking in a pair of pants?

There's no substitute for that moment when the jeans have given in to you, agreeing to curve where you curve, to lie flat and taut where you lie flat and taut. Unfortunately, there's no satisfactory shortcut to it, either. Many hot tips, some bordering on legend, are circulating: how Chicago kids fill the legs of new jeans with bricks, secure them at both ends, and drag them, tied to a car bumper, through city streets; how kids in Beverly Hills tie rocks to theirs and leave them for a few days at the bottom of a chlorinated swimming pool; how in lower Manhattan full-grown adults take fine sandpaper to their jeans' knees, seat, pocket edges, and crotch.

Nonetheless, ours remains a fast-moving society, so here's the best way to bleach jeans, softening them in the process and making them look, if not exactly older, at least less embarrassingly new.

First, avoid washing machines when you're using bleach; you can't see what's happening to the fabric, and uneven coloring may result. Instead, fill a bathtub with eight inches of warm water, enough to cover the jeans. Then add between a quart and a half gallon of bleach, depending on how much fading you're after and how much weakening of the cloth you're willing to tolerate. Stir to distribute the bleach evenly, then put in the jeans, laying them flat under the water and making sure they aren't twisted or folded in a way that will cause the bleach to work unevenly. Turn them over every five minutes, always making sure that there are no twists or folds. After a half-hour check for color (remember that any fabric looks darker when wet) and when it's right, remove them. Rinse thoroughly two or three times in fresh, cold water. Hang them to drip-dry so that the color won't run into folds.

When they're dry (assuming you've gotten them as light as you'd planned), you can machine wash them, using a fabric softener that will also cut the smell of the bleach. Then machine dry them. Don't be angry if they don't look quite the way indigo-dyed denim does when it's allowed to grow old naturally. That's another process, and it just can't be duplicated.

COMING TO TERMS

Most of the words we commonly use to refer to archetypally American blue jeans have specific foreign overtones. *Denim*, for instance, comes from the phrase *serge de Nîmes*, or cloth from Nîmes, the city in southern France where this heavy, sturdy fabric was loomed in the Middle Ages for the first time.

Dungarees, which many assume were so called because one could clean a barn in them, owe their identity to the town of Dhunga, India. Its seafaring inhabitants apparently favored a heavy denim fabric for their pants.

Jeans arrives via Genoa, Italy, where fifteenth-century sailors wore sturdy denim pants called *genes*, after their wearers. The word has since evolved to its present spelling. And that most famous Genoese Cristoforo Colombo is said to have used denim cloth for the sails that brought him to America.

America's contribution to etymology is, of course, Levi's, after Levi Strauss, who in 1850 began making pants for California gold miners, first from tent canvas, then finally out of denim that was dyed indigo blue. This word, unlike the others, is a trademark.

BEHIND THE SEAMS

A few facts of life concerning denim manufacturing can make you a more astute consumer.

First, big textile manufacturers like Burlington and Dan River make denim in mills that they own for the most part. Levi's, Blue Bell (makers of Wranglers), Lee, and the seventy-odd other domestic jean companies buy denim from these mills by the

The minimal solution: cotton jeans by Levi Strauss teamed with a cotton T-shirt.

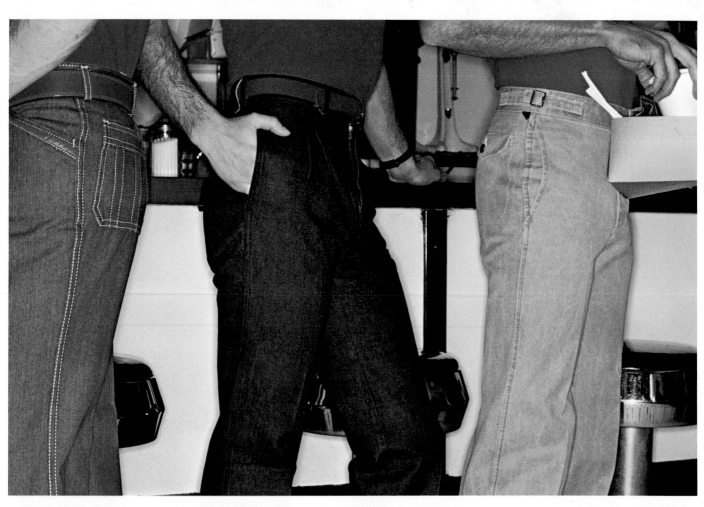

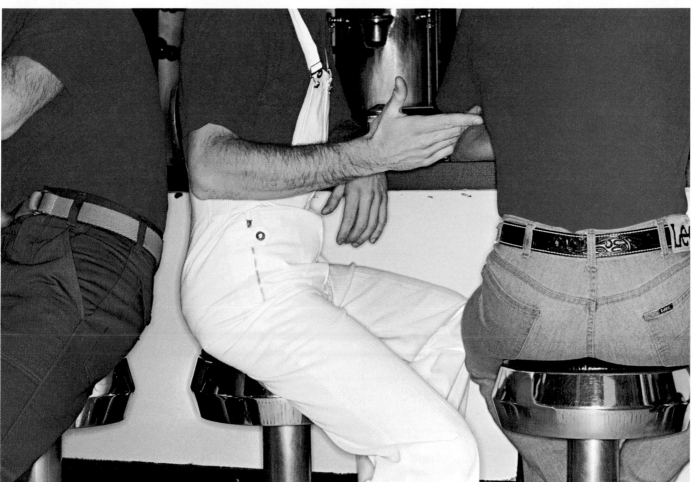

tens of millions of square yards. They then cut this denim to make blue jeans and related items.

Second, denim is not naturally blue. In fact, it starts out a pale natural color and, in some instances, actually goes through life that way. Most of the time, however, it's treated with indigo-blue dyes until it becomes the color we associate with the word *denim*.

Third, various other processes can be performed on the fabric, either before it's cut or afterward. For instance, it can be Sanforized, a control process that ensures shrinkage of no more than 1 percent, enabling manufacturers to cut exact sizes with complete accuracy.

Likewise, back at the mill, denim and polyester threads can be interwoven in either a 50/50 or 65/35 blend. This retards wrinkles and shrinkage and can also lend considerable structural strength. Blends account for roughly 10 percent of total denim sales.

LITTLE THINGS MEAN A LOT

Details count as much on jeans as on the most painstakingly tailored three-piece suit. However, most salespeople, even at stores specializing in jeans, aren't as knowledgeable about the intricacies of fit and dimensions as they might be. Using as examples the styles made by Levi's, the firm that has become synonymous with jeans, here's some guidance.

Above left: (from left to right) Cotton jeans trimmed in leather, from Spain; Italian-made tailored cotton jeans; cotton jeans from France.

Below left: (from left to right) Fatigue pants-inspired olive drab jeans; white cotton overalls from Canada; no-nonsense jeans in nylon-and-cotton.

In general, the basic jeans made by Levi's have already been preshrunk when you buy them. This means that if the pair you're trying on fits perfectly (well, maybe just a little tight, to suggest the body inside them), you buy them. They're guaranteed not to shrink more than 3 percent. The most basic Levi's are the number 505s. Look for these digits on the little leather patch sewn to the rear of the waistband, where you will also find the waist size and leg length. They're slightly tapered, eighteen inches in circumference at the knee and fifteen and three-quarter inches at the bottom. In addition, the basic jean category boasts a super-straight-legged model (number 519; seventeen and one-quarter inches at the knee and sixteen and three-quarter inches at the cuff) and two bell-bottom versions (number 646 with a twenty-one-inch bottom; number 684 with a full twenty-six inches, a significant difference to those who favor extra floppiness around the ankle).

In addition, there is a special jean that Levi's puts in its Western wear category, called the Saddleman boot jean, designed to give a particularly elegant fit over a pair of cowboy boots or any high boot with a prominent instep. This style, number 517, measures seventeen and one-quarter inches at the knee and nineteen and one-half inches at the cuff and is 100-percent preshrunk cotton. It has its fans, but it's not the purists' choice. That we've saved for last.

Unlike the other Levi's, the number 501s are *not* preshrunk and have to be bought *big*. An extra inch in the waist and an extra two inches in the inseam are the guidelines here, and if you don't observe them, you're going to wind up looking like you've raided your little brother's closet. These jeans have one other exclusive feature: a button, as opposed to a zipper, fly. Although some people are attracted to it, others can't be bothered buttoning when they can easily zip. If buying too big and dealing with buttons is too much for you, then forget the 501s and get the preshrunk 505s, which have, in essence, identical proportions and fit. It's that simple.

The contemporary tuxedo or dinner suit: a classic interpretation, though there are those who would question the use of satin facing at the cuffs, let alone a white cigarette holder. Note the cleanness of the look, the drama of white on black, the effectiveness of the glint of silver at the wrist.

CHAPTER 3
GOING FORMAL

Formality is a troubling word for some people, with its overtones of conformity, advance preparation, inhibition, and expenditure. Most of all, it implies (unlike such related words as *elegance* or *style*) a tacit agreement to abide by the rules. We'd like to be able to tell you that this isn't at all the case, that there's nothing more arduous or binding about full-dress weddings, diplomatic receptions, and charity balls than there is about barbecues; but we can't. Formal dress—and formal manners—continue to be areas in which one really *has* to know what he's doing.

There is one consolation, however. Although formal evenings require a high degree of commitment and docility on your part, and though they're no place for stragglers, nevertheless there's nothing vague or mysterious about them. In a sense, dressing for the office (see Chapter 2) is more challenging intellectually because then you really do have to assess who you are, how you come across, what your goals are, before you can leave the house. But when it comes to fancy dress, that's all

easy, because somebody else has done the work for you. It only remains to determine the degree of formality appropriate to the occasion and to honor it.

Traditionally, the subject of going formal has, Janus-like, looked in two directions: day and night. Daytime formal wear, once a staple in the wardrobes of even moderately prosperous urban gentlemen, has now been all but phased out of existence. When it is seen, it generally takes the form of the cutaway, a coat with tails extending to the backs of the knees, cut on a tapering line from the waist, single-breasted and secured by a solitary button. It's worn with striped trousers in shades of gray and black, and (for some very formal weddings and the like) a silk hat, ascot, and dove-gray gloves. The whole outfit is called morning dress (even when worn in the afternoon) and is to be reserved for occasions that will have terminated before six p.m.

With the exception of the occasional no-holds-barred wedding (or funeral, in which case a four-in-hand tie is substituted for the ascot), morning dress is reserved almost

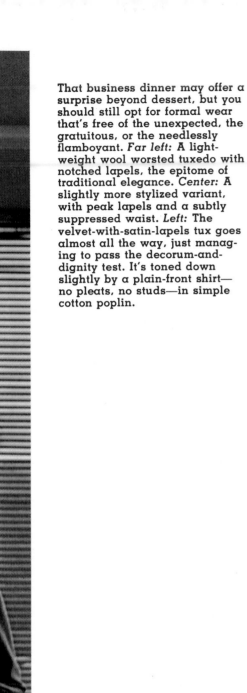

That business dinner may offer a surprise beyond dessert, but you should still opt for formal wear that's free of the unexpected, the gratuitous, or the needlessly flamboyant. *Far left:* A lightweight wool worsted tuxedo with notched lapels, the epitome of traditional elegance. *Center:* A slightly more stylized variant, with peak lapels and a subtly suppressed waist. *Left:* The velvet-with-satin-lapels tux goes almost all the way, just managing to pass the decorum-and-dignity test. It's toned down slightly by a plain-front shirt—no pleats, no studs—in simple cotton poplin.

exclusively for state or other highly official occasions. (It's what, for instance, Jimmy Carter refused to honor as the traditional Inauguration Day look.) Few, save members of the diplomatic corps and high-level government officials, are expected to own their own cutaways. On the very rare occasion that you might require one, renting is the accepted solution. But when you rent, make your arrangements far in advance and visit a reputable shop in possession of a good tailor. Nothing's more ludicrous than an ill-fitting cutaway or (its evening equivalent) tailcoat. Wearing either is an act of both bravura and rarefaction, and not to seem to be doing it all perfectly is to request derision from everyone else present.

Now about the tailcoat. It's what people mean when they say "white tie" and is, quite simply, the most formal outfit going, with the possible exception of the dress uniforms of rear admirals and five-star generals, few of whom we expect to be reading this. The tailcoat is required only rarely for some men, and never for most. It must be worn by both the father and the escort of a debutante at her coming out party, though not necessarily by the guests. It must be worn if an invitation specifies "white tie," as it might in the case of certain elaborate balls or diplomatic parties. And though it isn't out of place in a box at the opera or around a languorously lit, sumptuously laid table in a private dining room, it's hardly de rigueur even there. So don't plan on buying one, now or ever, unless you intend to achieve ambassadorial status or introduce a whole bevy of daughters to polite society. On the other hand, be aware that you can seem exceedingly dashing, and only slightly outre, by turning up in tails on a special night of nights and that a good formal-wear rental agency can outfit and tailor you satisfactorily for such a rhapsodic one-shot event.

That leaves us with the real staple of formal evenings. Most of us call it the tuxedo (after affluent Tuxedo Park, New York, where, in 1886, it made its first appearance), though "dinner jacket" is also commonly (and correctly) used. At any rate, it—and nothing else—is what's meant by black tie. And here, indeed, you should give considerable thought to the actual acquisition of one, at least if you're someone who enjoys living well or whose career is founded on an air of being able to do so. Quality and fit are all-important, of course, as they are with any suit. But a tuxedo should be thought of even more strongly as an investment. With any luck, no updating will have to be done for as many as five or six years, especially if you choose a suit of an essentially conservative cut. In this regard, single-breasted is always a safer bet than double; it can't possibly go out of fashion, though it may be temporarily overshadowed. Likewise, a notched lapel, though less dramatic than a peaked one, will never date you. (Shawl collars, in our opinion, are too redolent of the junior prom even to be considered by a man of style.)

Lapel facings are also a consideration, with satin the hardy perennial and velvet and grosgrain prominent options that fall into and out of favor almost cyclically.

Nor should that man of style we refer to neglect the aspect of dress called, a bit hatefully we admit, accessorizing. It counts for much of the impact of your self-presentation, virtually all of its subtlety, and nowhere more than in the formal-wear area. Because formal wear is so codified, omissions and exaggerations are going to be immediately evident and treated by onlookers as either bathetic gaffes or deliberate slaps in the face.

Of course, you'll need a black bow tie, of either the pre-tied (but not a clip-on!) or tie-it-yourself variety. We promise that no one will be able to tell the difference, if it's in a fabric that matches your lapel facings. And, if you're wearing a single-breasted tux, you'll also need a cummerbund or din-

DAYTIME

ANY SEMIFORMAL OCCASION

Coat	Single-breasted oxford gray jacket. (A groom might prefer a stroller or walking coat, basically the same oxford gray jacket but with satin edging on lapels, coat front, and pocket flaps.)
Trousers	Black-and-gray striped.
Waistcoat	In general, for a groom only. Gray, either single or double breasted.
Shirt	White, with a pleated front, spread collar, and French cuffs.
Tie	Gray striped silk four-in-hand.
	Black shoes and socks, gray gloves (optional), gold or silver jewelry.

FORMAL OCCASION

Coat	Oxford-gray cutaway, with plain or bound edges. Single breasted with either one or three buttons and either peaked or notched lapels, or double breasted with peaked lapels.
Trousers	Black-and-gray striped.
Waistcoat	Single or double breasted to match the coat or in a lighter shade of gray. (White is acceptable in summer.)
Shirt	White piqué with a wing collar and stiff or pleated front.
Tie	Gray striped silk four-in-hand. (A groom may prefer a gray-striped silk ascot.)
	Black shoes and socks, high silk hat, and gray or white gloves both optional. Pearl tie pin, if desired; gold, silver, or semiprecious stone cuff links. If an overcoat is needed, a black or oxford gray chesterfield is correct.

SEMIFORMAL (BLACK TIE) OCCASION

Coat   Black dinner jacket (also called a tuxedo). White, pastels, and the like appropriate from May to September, or throughout the year in tropical climates. Single or double breasted, with notched or peaked lapels or shawl collar.

Trousers   Black, with a side stripe; or, if the tuxedo jacket is of a deep color other than black, of that same color.

Waistcoat   Black satin, to match the jacket's lapel facings. But cummerbunds are perhaps more common and are also more comfortable in warm weather. (Never wear anything but a cummerbund with a white or pastel dinner jacket.) With a double-breasted model, neither waistcoat nor cummerbund is necessary. With any model, you may wish to wear suspenders, as tuxedo pants are generally beltless.

Shirt   Pleated, tucked, or ruffled formal shirt, in white, beige, light blue, or other gentle colors. Traditional collar and French cuffs. (Some wing collar shirts are occasionally seen with tuxes.)

Tie   Black satin, velvet, or grosgrain. The idea is to match the lapel facings.

Shoes are of black calfskin or patent leather, socks of black nylon or silk. Jewelry is gold or platinum, silver or semiprecious stone, almost anything that's elegant and to your liking. Just make sure the various pieces match, i.e., are *all* of gold or silver. A black chesterfield overcoat is ideal. Dark cashmere or even tweed is acceptable.

FORMAL OCCASION

Coat   Black tailcoat with satin or grosgrain lapels.

Trousers   Same fabric as coat, with satin side stripes.

Waistcoat   Single-breasted white piqué. *No* cummerbund.

Shirt   White piqué front with wing collar and French cuffs. (Avoid the archaic starched or stiff look here; it's no longer necessary.)

Tie   White piqué bow.

Shoes are of black calfskin or patent leather, either lace-up or pumps. Socks are of black silk or nylon. Jewelry should be of platinum or pearl; gold is jarring here, too bright. Gloves are white, in leather or cloth. A high silk hat is an option, a cane a bit of an affectation, but try it if you think you can carry it off. Again, the black chesterfield overcoat is ideal. A white silk scarf is always appropriate.

ner vest in the same fabric and color as the tie. With a double-breasted model, nothing need be done to ceremonialize the midsection. A pleated-front, white formal-dress shirt (or perhaps one in a light color though frankly it's hard to beat the contrast that a bright white shirt will offer the blackness of your suit and tie), requiring closure with pearl or black onyx studs along the front and cuff links at the wrist, black silk suspenders, black tie shoes in either calf or patent leather, gray gloves, and a white silk scarf complete a virtually unimpeachable picture.

We haven't mentioned pants. Of course, they match the jacket (the tuxedo is, after all, a suit) and have that very stylized stripe down the leg in a fabric that carries out the theme of the lapel facing. But we've saved them till last to make a seasonal point. The pants don't, you see, match the jacket at all during the summer months *if* you follow the time-honored dictate that, once the weather's turned warm, only a white linen dinner

If there's an argument to be made for the white dinner jacket, this—and not the timid, baggy thing you wore to the junior prom—is it. All silk and, take it from us, very expensive. (You can't see them, but those are black trousers he's wearing.)

Right: We can only assume by this couple's utter formality that a truly important evening lies ahead. "Tails," with satin lapel and leg stripe, a wing collar shirt, and cotton piqué tie and vest.

Below: A double-breasted tux, the height of suavity. Wool with satin lapels. The bow tie is likewise satin, to match the satin facings.

Formal wear rules are very clear-cut. Thus, there's little room for choice. Individuality must enter the evening by way of accessories. Your look can scale the very heights of elegance or cling to the traditional tenets of unruffled propriety. Just how brightly you'll care to glow in the dark is totally up to you.

(1) Satin top hat. (2) Capeskin gloves. (3) Walking stick. (4) Dress socks. (5) Grosgrain ribboned formal shoes. (6) Cuff links with basket-weave motif. (7) Calfskin belt. (8) 18-karat gold pillbox. (9) 18-karat gold cigarette case. (10) Cuff links and studs. (11) 14-karat gold cuff links. (12) Vermeil pen. (13) 18-karat gold studs. (14) Onyx cuff links and studs. (15) Cigarette holder. (16) Gold-and-onyx cuff links. (17) White gold-and-onyx ring. (18) 18-karat gold watch fob. (19) Pocket watch. (20) 14-karat gold lighter.

Weddings are perhaps the one genuinely formal occasion in one's life. On this page, betrotheds who already seem to have more than their share of problems are playing their roles to the hilt. In the photo above, the groom at a daytime wedding wears a grey Dacron-and-worsted cutaway with matching waistcoat and coordinated striped trousers. A white, wing-collared, polyester-and-cotton shirt and a black-and-silver-striped ascot complete the picture. Note the silk top hat that he wears and the gloves he holds, both being integral to his outfit.

The photograph on the right, merely a potentially flammable situation, is rendered a bit less shocking because, well, at least it's nighttime. The groom wears a worsted tailcoat and high-waisted trousers. Accessories include white gloves, top hat (in hand), and patent-leather slipons. A carnation provides the finishing touch for both him and his best man.

jacket will do. This rule is something to take seriously; however, while it makes sense to wear light colors when it's hot, you should also know that, more and more, the black dinner jacket is achieving a certain year-round legitimacy, at least in big cities. White dinner jackets are, of course, still the thing on dressy Caribbean cruises and at mid-July country-club dances, but more and more (perhaps because of their association with such activities) they seem downright older-generation. For this reason, coupled with the fact that tuxedos are now being made in a variety of truly lightweight wool and mohair worsteds and that few, if any, truly formal occasions arise during the hottest months of the year, we advise that you hold off on purchasing anything but your basic black dinner suit, at least till you've seen what's done by others in your region, community, and social stratum.

The most trying aspect of formal affairs is knowing what to wear when. No single outfit is applicable for all formal occasions. The time of day and season are still significant, as are the nature of the event itself, and the

We've included these two shots to illustrate a point we began to make earlier. Obviously, neither man is wearing what has been defined as formal wear: no tuxedo, no cutaway, no tailcoat. No bow ties, white or black. But spend a little time here. You'll see that in each case, a feeling of considerable formality (not just elegance or dressiness) has been engendered by the nature of the clothing itself, its obvious quality and fit; by the way it's been accessorized with shirts, ties, and pocket squares of muted and subtle hue; and by the spirit in which the stuff is being worn: a certain self-confidence is evident. But more than that, there is an awareness that this is, whatever else, a big night, and that things are going to be done right, with no corners cut, no pointless deviations.

At far left, **a velvet suit, supplemented by that most resonant of personal luxuries, an all-silk shirt.** *At left,* **the George V Hotel in Paris, one definition of high style, is countered by another: a suit-and-shirt combination by Yves Saint Laurent, who's come to epitomize the French penchant for elegant innovation.**

role one is playing in it. (As you've seen, a groom's attire can differ slightly from that of the male wedding guests.) Keep in mind that six p.m. remains the line of demarcation between daytime and evening occasions, though whether or not it's dark outside is what really counts. Likewise, while summer formal attire is correctly worn in the northern portions of the country only between, roughly, Memorial Day and Labor Day, it's certainly in evidence in Jacksonville, Florida; Dallas, and Los Angeles whenever the weather is warm enough to lend credence to its tropical aura.

Depending on where and how you live, you may be additionally surprised and a little relieved to discover that the ambience of at least *some* black tie evenings has changed radically. At certain New York gatherings, for instance, the invitations to which specify black tie, just as they would have fifty years ago, it's not unusual to see men (and fairly urbane ones, at that) in anything from full-dress white tie and tails down through the technically correct (at least in this case) tuxedo to dark and dignified three-piece suits, blazers, and even the occasional tweed jacket. Does anyone feel out of place? Perhaps, but for the most part, they don't show it.

This doesn't necessarily mean that you can break the rules and flout the conventions, but it does suggest that, if your life is a relaxed or slightly unconventional one, you can, in some situations, stretch them until they fit comfortably. The lack of a tuxedo and cummerbund needn't keep you from enjoying a certain kind of black tie evening, and you shouldn't let it. Do attempt to do the occasion justice by reaching for the navy blazer, so easily made to seem if not exactly dressy then at least distinguished, rather than grabbing the old herringbone-with-suede-elbow-patches. And do polish your shoes and consider wearing your sleekest white shirt. Exercise your judgment about the situation at hand, but if you can help it, don't stay home. That's no way to have fun—or to do business.

CHAPTER 4
TRAVELING RIGHT

The art of traveling today is essentially one of miniaturization. How else to deal with the ever-present discipline of airline size restrictions on the one hand and the fact that trips (especially for business purposes) are becoming shorter and more frequent, on the other? There is a whole new school of international dressing based on the exigencies of simplicity, interchangeability, and good taste. In short, it has become necessary to look better and better on ever-shorter notice and within the confines of a very limited space—your suitcase.

Consider simplicity first. When packing for any kind of departure, whether it's a pleasure trip to Europe or a quick dash to a plant in Grand Rapids, the same rule prevails. Never take anything that is too complexly patterned or incongruously colored. Zero in on the suit or two that you're taking, then build up a repertory of items keyed to their color.

Next consider the concept of interchangeability. Here again the facts are eloquent in their directness. Everything that goes into your suitcase should be coordinated with everything else. Period.

The next item, taste, is more ambiguous. What is taste, who has it, and in this case is it international? To the last the answer is very definitely yes. A standard does exist, recognized throughout most of the West, East, or third world, which is based on a limited number of easily recognized symbols—the navy blazer, for instance, or the crisp white shirt, clothes that, incidentally, fulfill the other two requirements of our list. When it comes to traveling, however, the element of daring that is so integral to the exercise of taste should be checked. You're not trying to be unique, remember, just simple and elegant.

On the following pages you will find suggestions for three complete wardrobes for one-week visits to Europe, to a tropical resort, and to a temperate climate on a business trip. But first, let's start with three staples of any man's travel wardrobe—the gray flannel suit, the navy blazer, and the trench coat—which will carry you beautifully through practically any travel situation.

It seems to us that the gray flannel suit—and why not make it three-piece at the same time—could well serve as a keystone to any man's travel strategy. It is, of course, discreet enough to match with virtually anything else in your wardrobe, and at the same time it reflects a feeling of stability, important when you want to make a quick but lasting impression. Here it is in wool, complete with vest and peaked lapels, and accessorized with a silk tie, pocket handkerchief, and a subdued check shirt.

Above: The trench coat is one of the few positive outgrowths of World War I; Burberry's classic originated as a protection for doughboys at the front. These days, it has become an ideal travel garment. You can carry it on the plane over your arm, and it equips you, elegantly, for almost any exigency.

Left: The blazer hardly needs to be explained; it stands today as *the* all-around wardrobe essential. There's virtually no dressy occasion where it can't be worn, short of formal events; yet its sportive Edwardian origins enable it to blend smoothly into situations where no one else is wearing a jacket. Surely the embodiment of versatility, the blazer doubles for banker's hours as well as three-day weekends. Here it's shown with an exceptional number of period trimmings, executed in wool serge, with brass buttons—and it's double-breasted.

EUROPEAN PLAN

Packing for any trip is somewhat traumatic. Too many mistakes or mismatches and you'll find yourself on the rue de Rivoli at 9 A.M. waiting for the stores to open. But there is an art to it all. It's what you leave behind that's crucial when it comes to effective packing. A week in Europe should be a triumph of condensation. Starting with a safari jacket that has a double life—it's reversible—here's how to do it.

TAKE THESE

1 reversible safari jacket	1 pair of dress shoes
1 sport coat	1 tie
3 pairs of trousers	1 pocket square
3 shirts	7 pairs of underwear
2 sweaters	7 pairs of socks
	2 belts

First impressions are important, so when you take off on your trip, combine a reversible safari jacket in cotton chino/flannel with Dacron-and-cotton trousers, a striped shirt, and a silk tie for a slightly formal, very pulled-together look.

The ideal wardrobe is adaptable to many situations. The unobtrusive plaid jacket is teamed up with a cashmere turtleneck and, again, the flannel trousers.

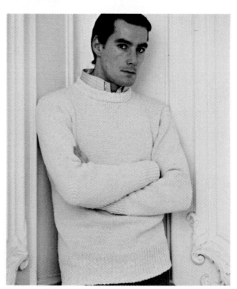

Above: A subtle plaid jacket is sufficiently formal to meet that European sense of propriety, but relaxed enough to carry you through the leisure hours. It's in wool and is teamed with a pair of flannel trousers, a cotton shirt, and a leather belt. *Below:* Keeping the color spectrum low-keyed is vital when it comes to wardrobe stretching. So add a cotton crew-necked sweater.

The reversible safari jacket, with matching trousers
and shirt, works beautifully as a suit. The jacket is in
cotton chino/flannel, the trousers in flannel, and the
shirt in cotton.

Right: The cotton sweater is mated with a cotton shirt
and the cashmere turtleneck as well as Dacron-and-
cotton trousers, to create another ready-to-go look.

White should form the foundation of your resort collection. *Left:* A white cotton poplin jacket worn with white cotton poplin trousers. *Right:* A double-breasted rayon blazer works with another pair of cotton poplin trousers, a white button-down shirt, a tie, and a hat. *Far right:* The same neutral-colored trousers meet an easy sweater and a white silk scarf. *Below:* A white cotton voile top worn with the white poplin trousers seen at left.

CARIBBEAN HIDEAWAY

Whatever time of year you plan your escape, a trip to the sun should be carefree. And the last thing you want to worry about is whether your wardrobe fits the bill. So here's a minilexicon of wearables for every contingency.

TAKE THESE

1 double-breasted blazer	1 sweatshirt	1 pair of sneakers
1 safari jacket	1 lounging outfit	1 tie
2 pairs of trousers	1 tennis outfit	1 scarf
1 pair of shorts	1 swimsuit	4 pairs of underwear
1 dress shirt	1 pair of dress shoes	4 pairs of socks
2 T-shirts	1 pair of espadrilles	2 pairs of sunglasses
1 sweater		

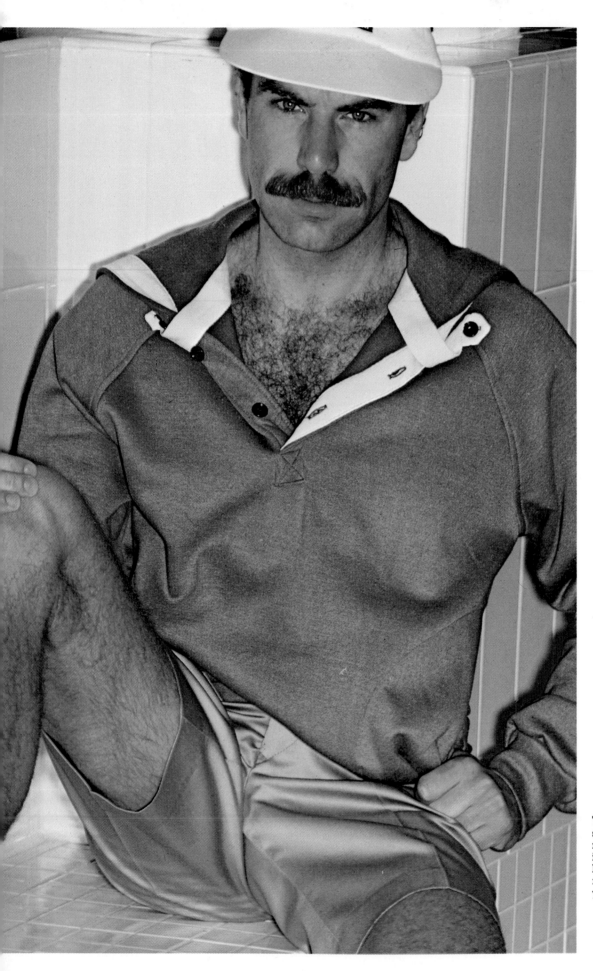

The once-humble
sweatshirt now
makes a statement of
its own. Its good
looks and practicality
merit its inclusion in
your sun wardrobe.

Left: Simplicity is the key to compactness. Stripes are fine, but avoid prints. And throw in a slicker for good measure. *Below, left:* A fortrel-and-terry plaid swimsuit. Pack one, at least. *Center:* The game's the same wherever you play it, and you'll want to look the part—so pack a tennis outfit. *Right:* The navy blazer adds authority to a striped cotton shirt and the cotton poplins.

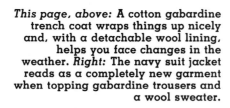

Opposite page, left: **The classic cornerstone: a three-piece navy wool suit garnished with a discreet shirt and tie.** *Right:* **Minus its vest, the navy suit yields yet another look when worn with a striped shirt.**

This page, above: A cotton gabardine trench coat wraps things up nicely and, with a detachable wool lining, helps you face changes in the weather. *Right:* The navy suit jacket reads as a completely new garment when topping gabardine trousers and a wool sweater.

BUSINESS WEEK

Going out of town, this time on business. Whether it's something really serious, like a job interview, or something a little lighter, say, a conference on laser beams, the prerequisites for a week of traveling are the same: a sane, practical wardrobe packing sufficient flexibility to carry you through after-hours activities.

TAKE THESE

1 three-piece suit	4 ties
1 sport coat	1 pocket handkerchief
1 pair of trousers	4 pairs of underwear
1 trench coat	4 pairs of socks
3 shirts	1 briefcase
3 sweaters	1 pair of glasses
1 pair of dress shoes	

Left: A double-breasted wool sweater is useful for both business and entertaining, especially when teamed with the gabardine trousers, a light-toned shirt, and a scarf. *Bottom:* Enter the silk sport coat, combining the virtues of working luxury with leisure style. The same shirt and sweater shown on the previous page add up to a whole new dimension.

Throwing the rule book away gives another life to the silk sport coat. It's worked in with the trousers from the suit shown previously, and a final addition, a shetland sweater, completes the transition.

PACKING IT ALL IN

The chances are fairly good, given the dramatic swiftness with which we seem to be handling business and personal decisions today, that most of your trips will be planned at the last moment. We're also willing to bet on your not having much more than an hour to pack on the average. All this makes it imperative that you have a handy, instant-activator buried in your memory to deal with the problem of what to put in your suitcase and where to put it. Care and technique are what's required. So here are a few pointers to keep you in small (and large) changes.

☐ Heavy items go at the bottom of the case, resting on the hinges at the back (shoes, etc.). They'd eventually shift to that position anyway, so why not put them there in the first place to avoid disturbing everything else?

☐ Distribute weight evenly from side to side for balanced carrying. For instance, pack two pairs of shoes opposite each other; pack four pairs by placing one pair in each corner of the suitcase.

☐ Cushion each fabric fold with the fold of another fabric (the old "tissue" idea) to

Left: **A polyester-and-linen three-piece suit, teamed with those two traveler's indispensables: a good raincoat, lightweight and capable of taking a beating, and a no-nonsense briefcase, in this instance of canvas-and-leather construction.**

ward off wrinkles. Use your rolled-up crushable items—underwear, socks, pajamas—between folds.

□ Divide garments into sections—shirts and pajamas in one area, ties and handkerchiefs in another. Then keep sections separate by placing each category of clothes into its own plastic bag. This method results in firmer packing and fewer wrinkles; it also protects clothes from dirt. Another bonus: customs inspectors will go faster when everything is separated and clearly visible.

□ Spillables and aerosol cans should go into your grooming kit. Unstable pressure conditions (especially in airplane baggage compartments) can cause problems, so it's better to keep grooming items separate from clothes.

□ Don't pack your grooming kit into the suitcase you're going to check. Keep it with you. If your luggage should be misplaced, you'll still be able to keep yourself well groomed in the interim.

□ When packing a suit, never button the coat. It won't lie flat if you do.

□ Carry several inflatable plastic hangers with you. They're inexpensive (about 60 cents each) and invaluable for drip-dry or wash-and-wear garments.

□ Pack your shoes in plastic bags or shoe mittens. They'll keep dirt away from your clothes.

□ To save space, if space-saving is a consideration, stuff your socks into your shoes—which also serves as a good replacement for shoe trees.

□ If you're saving something new to wear on your trip, don't. Wear it beforehand, then wash it or have it cleaned.

□ Don't be afraid to pack your luggage tightly. If everything is carefully folded and rolled into a tightly packed suitcase, there's no chance of clothes getting crushed or loose items shifting around.

With the foregoing tips in mind, follow this rundown of crushproof ways to pack individual apparel items:

Hats. Stuff the crown of the hat with "crushables" (i.e., underwear and the like), then pack more crushables around the crown and brim.

Shirts. Put each shirt (as it comes folded from the laundry) into its own plastic bag (a Baggie is fine) after removing all the cardboard. Next, stack each shirt, alternating the collars so you'll have a compact rectangular package. Keeping shirts this way, even after you've arrived at your destination, makes it easier to get at them.

Ties. Carry them in a tie case. Or make your own with two pieces of cardboard (from your shirts) cut the length of a folded-over tie; and then sandwich your ties between the pieces of cardboard. Ties can also be rolled up tight. By stretching them taut and smooth in a roll, wrinkles are avoided and the rolls can be used to fill up odd corners of your bag.

Belts. Roll them by sticking the end through the buckle and then curling the end inward. The belt will coil tight and won't jiggle loose.

Socks. Roll each pair together from toe to top until it looks like a fat Tootsie Roll.

Shoes. Shoes are the pivotal item in deciding how to arrange clothes in a suitcase. There are several methods—all effective. One is to put all your clothes in the suitcase, then stick your shoes at the ends with soles toward the sides of the bag. Placing one pair at each end is most advantageous for easy carrying. Another technique, if you're only taking one pair, is to place the soles along the hinge end of the luggage (which becomes the bottom when standing upright). For two pairs, place the shoes sole to heel—also along the hinge end. Still another way is to put shoes in the bottom of the luggage first, and then pack everything else over them. Once you arrange the shoes and major items of apparel, fill in the holes with your rolled-up crushables.

Underwear. Fold undershirt and shorts (each of them) in thirds lengthwise. Place the shorts inside the undershirt and roll them up together.

Suits. Step-by-step directions for two ways to pack a suit follow:

Packing the two-suiter with no suit frame. Remove the hangers and place both pairs of pants on the bottom (with the waistbands arranged vertically against each other), allowing the pants legs to hang over both sides of the case. Arrange the jackets on hangers (fold the arms in toward the center; leave the bottom buttons open on the jackets) and hook them on the posts in the center.

Fold the pants one over the other.

Fold the jackets up over the pants.

Packing the one-suiter with suit frame. Open the fixture and place it on a flat surface.

Place the suit on the hanger and lock the hanger onto the hanger post. Fold the jacket sleeves half under and half over the side of the jacket.

Fold the bottom of the frame upward to the top.

Place the suit in the case so that the tail of the jacket faces the bottom of the case.

Sport Coat. To pack a jacket in an ordinary flat suitcase, try the inside-out method. First pull the collar up, then fold the shoulders back so they touch, checking to see that the seams are carefully aligned. With one hand from inside one shoulder, grasp both shoulders and flip the jacket inside out. Be certain that the sleeves lie straight inside the material. Fold the jacket over double to fit in the luggage.

Slacks. When packing a flat suitcase, trousers can be folded or rolled. To roll, first place slacks on a flat surface. Roll them up tightly from the bottom, pulling the seams out taut as you roll. If you prefer folding, fold the slacks over another garment—a jacket, for example, or insert tissue paper inside the fold.

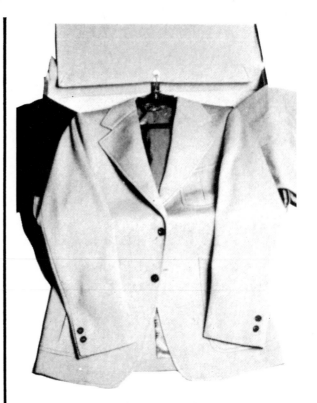

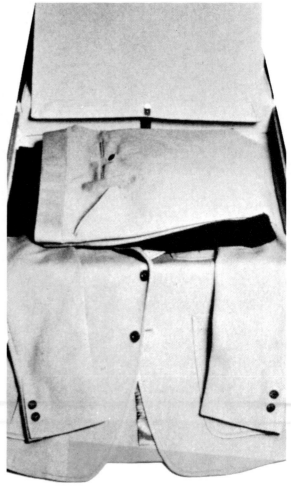

How to pack the two-suiter with no suit frame. *Right, above:* Jacket and pants arranged over case. *Below:* Pants folded over. *Far right:* Jacket folded over pants.

THE PERMANENT TRAVEL KIT

To pack a grooming kit anew each time you're preparing to travel is an invitation to forget a needed item. The answer, clearly, is maintaining a permanent kit, with everything prepacked and kept in readiness. Basically, here's what should be included in the well-stocked case: razor and package of blades (or electric razor and recharger, if you prefer, for longer trips); shave foam or cream; after shave; talcum and powder puff for it; toothbrush (in case) and paste; aspirin; comb (unbreakable); deodorant; shampoo; hair groom or spray (if used); toe and fingernail clippers; styptic pencil; bandages (one of each size); two collar stays. Naturally, these items may not fit into a case in their regular sizes; so buy the smallest sizes of everything you can, and glom (free) sample bottles of others from department stores. Or buy little plastic bottles at a variety store (about 25 cents apiece) and label them. These containers hold about a two-week supply of whatever you put in. It's best to store razors empty. An exposed blade is dangerous, for one thing; and moisture in the closed case corrodes and dulls the edge, so you'd have to replace it anyway. To fill small bottles from large ones, use a lady's perfume funnel, but don't store it in the case. Also, don't fill bottles to the top or they may leak into the case. A powder puff serves two purposes: it keeps powder off your host's floor and acts as an absorbent should something leak. The advantage of plastic over glass bottles is that they don't tend to leak and, of course, won't break if they drop. The case is your choice.

CHAPTER 5

SURPLUS AND SURVIVAL WEAR

Innovation is the blood relative of adversity. The current upheaval in the way we put together casual wardrobes has a lot to do with the economic and social tailspins of the seventies. With that in mind, it would seem that the eruption of the survival aesthetic, first among the avant-garde but increasingly in mainstream America, is actually a perfectly normal reaction to the exigencies of a situation in which the expectations of the Western world have been turned upside down. Considering that fashion has always been a sensitive barometer of the state of the world, it follows that the current global turmoil should have had such vital repercussions on our wardrobes.

Perhaps fashion isn't quite the word for all of what's happening. It needs more aggressive nomenclature, something that connotes the sheer resourcefulness of it all. There is a definite military overtone to the survival look, and although it's risky to compare the act of putting yourself together every morning with the ruthless dexterity necessary for storming a beachhead, there is a link. The direction dressing has taken

lately has implications beyond the mere act of fabricating an image that's in step with the times. It's part of a fresh way of looking at the world.

Whatever the causes, the look is fast becoming ubiquitous, at least in more fashion-conscious areas of the country. Its hallmarks have spread beyond clothes and involve such adjuncts as short hair, a beard and/or mustache—also kept short—and a defiant mien. The *de rigueur* stance is cool, aloof, and distant.

In France and other parts of Europe the movement has acquired political overtones. In Paris it has become a convention, if not indeed a necessity, to tie a peasant kerchief around your wrist, stuff your army shirt into flannel breeches, and stomp around in mud-caked boots to prove your membership in the avant-garde. Third-world solidarity is the chic slogan here; the French are flocking to buy the sort of coarse, quilted jackets that make so much sense in or out of the rice paddies of the sixteenth arondissement, and are of course endowed with the price of a designer shirt.

The real thing: an army flight suit that doubles as multipurpose sports gear. Hike, jog, or sail away in it. Velcro fasteners add a note of applied technology, letting you adjust the suit's size.

A cotton gabardine suit based on an army original, worn with a regulation army belt and canvas boots.

The construction boot faces the seventies in a fresh shade, olive drab.

But fashion also dovetails with life-style in Europe, in a sophisticated fusion not known in this country. So survival wear in France is tied into all those glossy exhortations from Italian shelter magazines to redo your living room with a limited number of crucial items from the Hanoi People's Department Store and with the import of sackcloth shirts from Bangladesh that look like floor plans for a temple honoring minimalism.

How to identify the survival look? A key difference is shape. Clothes are almost draped rather than worn. And natural fabrics are elected to get the message across. Often these are coarse weaves in earth tones but unequivocally bristly fabrics are usually avoided, however. Looking too self-consciously humble would defeat the latently aggressive posture of survival. This new sensibility depends on re-created reality, a sort of poetic distortion rather than the honest article.

One of the movement's basic tenets involves never buying anything in your own size. This practice breaks down into two handy subcategories. If the item is new, buy it a size larger; if it's surplus, take a size smaller. It's all a matter of tailoring. Clothes available secondhand are largely military gear and fit the body quite snugly. Bought a shade smaller, they provide a perfect primal layer. A new garment, on the other hand, if you're really au courant, will most likely be dolman- or raglan-sleeved or at least cut with generosity. Buying a larger size allows room for other goings-on—i.e., several other layers of clothes.

If the upper half of your body is covered by one easy-wrap garment, then the lower

Right: **The rise of down. A navy blue jacket stuffed with northern down, worn with a beige cotton shirt and beige corduroy trousers.**

Far right: **Adding another element to the outfit readies you for cross-country trekking. A beige belted coat with a wealth of details in Dacron and cotton.**

portion of you will be bursting with as many bits of engineering as a spare-parts manual. Zippers, pockets, loops, Velcro fasteners: the entire battery of applied technology will be present. Of course, it's all in the name of functionalism, in the tradition of self-help gadgetry initially espoused by the *Whole Earth Catalog*. The theory almost seems to be that if you were stranded on a lonely road without spare parts for your motor, you could improvise with the paper clips, old bicycle chains, and Swiss army knives that you just happened to have with you in your revised-design, carpenter-type, seagoing, land-roving fatigue pants. Denims will do in a pinch, but you really ought to have them in used army green.

Comparison-shop the relative merits of, say, Finnish or Portuguese army-issue boots. Otherwise settle for a streamlined canvas-and-rubber reproduction. Don't get hung up on authenticity, by the way, since no one's going to care if it's not the real thing. After all, this is fashion we're talking about.

If the new sensibility is based on a foundation of fantasy and half-digested ideological programs, can it really claim to be a valid direction? The answer is yes. Fashion only deals metaphorically with the issues of our time, and it's certainly no secret that even the most artless simplicity requires some degree of art. It's a little contrary, of course, but since that's the way of the world at the moment, it could be considered indicative of fashion's reflective capabilities.

The essence of current thinking, then, is that the eclectic mixes now being concocted and worn, the judicious blends of half a dozen societies all shaken up together, have as their ultimate goal the creation of a style that's absolutely free. Although based on a significantly narrow yet infinitely adaptable range of choices, the look is ultimately capable, with minor modifications, of serving a variety of uses from business to pleasure. Clothes are obviously ceasing to be a codified uniform and are becoming instead a system of spare parts that can combine to form any number of variations.

Opposite page, left: **Polyester-and-cotton twill shorts, polyester-and-cotton shirt, and a stretch belt.** *Right:* **Trevira-and-cotton shorts and a Dacron-and-cotton shirt. Both are worn with knee socks.**

Below: **A polyester and cotton overshirt with a corduroy collar lined in tartan wool serves as an excellent foil to a beefy wool shirt. A turtleneck completes the layering.**

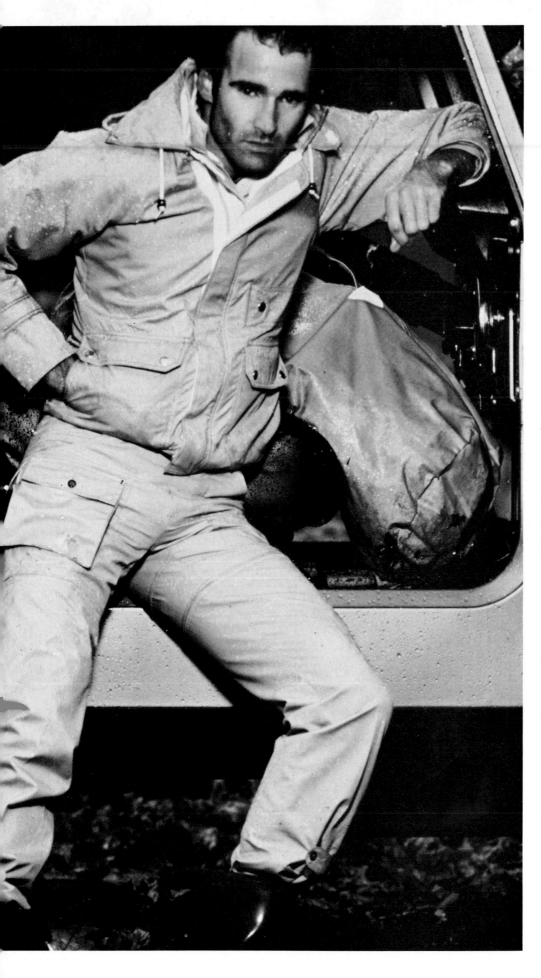

Far left: The functional tradition (continued). A cotton denim jumpsuit with cargo pockets.

Left: A fair deal for foul weather. Ostensibly a rain outfit, this is actually a miniwardrobe. A reversible rain jacket in silicone-treated cotton with removable hood. Add convertible rain pants (the legs zip off to become shorts) and you have a foolproof, watertight look.

Below: Minimal thinking is the shortest distance between two fashion points. These cotton poplin shorts with orange leg trim and industrial zippers double as swimwear.

Whatever we choose to make of survival wear's popularity, as a reflection of sex or politics, or as the beginnings of fashion fascism and a disquieting omen of things to come, the visual evidence is right before our eyes in increasing numbers, an expression of the intensity and ambiguity of our age.

Yet there is a contradictory theme underlying the impulse toward the other chic, a kind of dualism about our feelings that is perhaps summed up in Fulke Greville's statement on the essential conflict between life (and fashion, need we add?) published in 1699.

Oh wearisome Condition of Humanity!
Borne under one law, to another bound;
Vainely begot, and yet forbidden vanity,
Created sick, commanded to be sound;
What meaneth Nature by these diverse
   Lawes?
Passion and Reason, self-division cause.

PUTTING IT ALL TOGETHER:
WARDROBE STRATEGY FOR EVERY PRICE RANGE

Wardrobe strategy has never been more important. Inflation may be leveling off, but chances are your paycheck still has some catching up to do. To make things a little easier, we've come up with six possible scenarios for dressing well, showing you how you can put together a complete wardrobe of clothes similar to the ones you've just seen in Chapters 1 through 5. Within three price ranges—low, medium, and high—we've assembled two separate wardrobes. One is dressy, the other casual. The goal, however, is maximum flexibility. After all, it's not just the price of an item that counts, but the way it works with everything in your wardrobe.

$400 CASUAL

$16
Denim fatigue-style pants (A).

$40
Leather slip-on shoes (C).

$40
Donegal-tweed pants (B).

$20
Wool-cotton-and-linen scarf (D).

$21
Wool-and-nylon outer shirt (E).

$16
Polyester-and-rayon plaid shirt (F).

$17
Acrylic-and-wool sweater (G).

$5
Silk pocket square (H).

$16
Polyester-and-cotton shirt (J).

$16
Denim jeans (I).

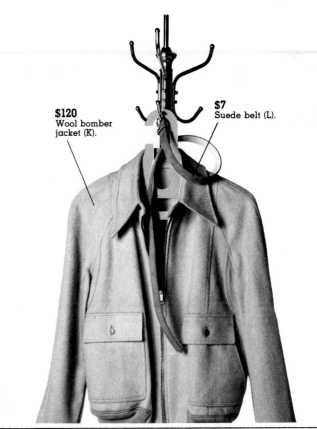

$120
Wool bomber jacket (K).

$7
Suede belt (L).

$16
Orlon sweater (N).

$10
Wool hat (P).

$7
Wool-and-leather gloves (O).

$33
Wool tweed vest (M).

Sense and sensibility are what count here. Take a catalytic item—in this case, a bomber jacket—then key the colors and textures of every other item to it. The result: a repertory of great flexibility and infinite possibilities, enabling your clothes to lead double and even triple lives as part of an interchangeable system.

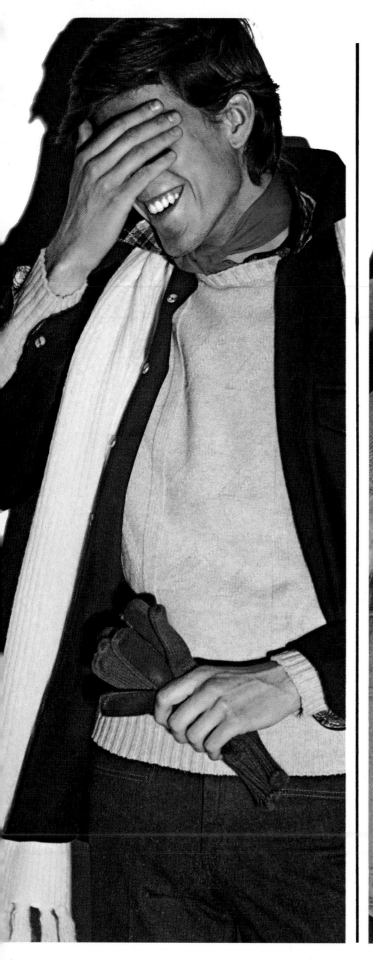

Opposite page, far left: Multiplication is the name of the game. The components are the handkerchief (H), plaid shirt (J), sweater (G), outer shirt (E), jeans (I), scarf (D), and gloves (O). *Left:* The bomber jacket (K), tweed vest (M), and plaid shirt (F).

This page, top left: Fluidly blended with tweed pants (B) are hooded sweater (N), scarf (D), and plaid shirt (F), topped off with hat (P) and underscored with shoes (C). *Top right:* Pants (A), bomber jacket (K), sweater (G), outer shirt (E), and handkerchief (H). *Bottom left:* The outer shirt (E) relaxes with fatigue pants (A), belt (L), and sweater (G). *Right:* The outer shirt (E) assumes a jacket role when worn over plaid shirt (J), while denim jeans (I) keep it simple and a handkerchief (H) adds a splash of color.

$400 DRESSY

Your business sense tells you that a good appearance bodes well for an upwardly mobile professional life, but you've got other commitments too. So this neatly planned dressy wardrobe should see you through your workday and leave some leeway for after hours.

$18
Polyester crepe shirt (A).

$85
Wool-and-nylon sport jacket (B).

$35
Wool-and-nylon trousers (C).

$46
Kidskin shoes (F).

$5
Silk pocket square (G).

$150
Polyester-and-wool suit (E).

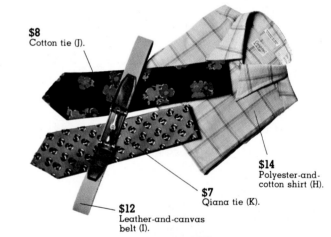

$8
Cotton tie (J).

$14
Polyester-and-cotton shirt (H).

$7
Qiana tie (K).

$12
Leather-and-canvas belt (I).

$14
Acrylic sweater (D).

The suit (E) is, of course, at the center of the game plan. Here it's teamed with a shirt (H), tie (J), and pocket square (G) to form a logical partnership.

Above left: The sport coat (B) works with the trousers (C) to pull together a crisp business look that also includes shirt (A) and tie (K). Shoes (F), belt (I), and pocket square (G) complete the picture. *Above right (top picture):* The suit (E) minus vest acquires the sweater (D) and shirt (A) to create a more relaxed feeling. *Above right (bottom picture):* Shirt (A) and sweater (D) are mated with pocket square (G) and trousers (C). *Right:* The sport coat (B) joins the vest and pants from the suit (D) and shirt (A) and tie (K) to provide an alternate way to work.

$ 700 CASUAL

$90
Sweater made in Italy (F).

$30
Suede-and-rope shoes with crepe soles (E).

$65
Wool-and-nylon trousers (G).

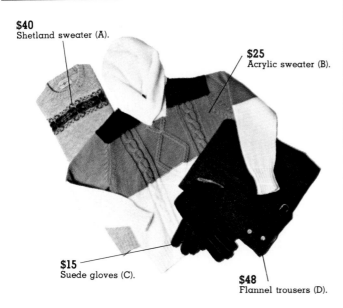

$40
Shetland sweater (A).

$25
Acrylic sweater (B).

$15
Suede gloves (C).

$48
Flannel trousers (D).

$70
Wool sweater (H).

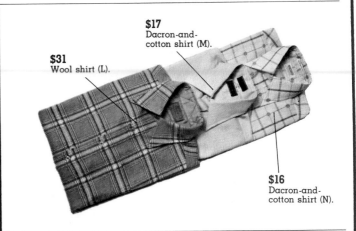

$17
Dacron-and-cotton shirt (M).

$31
Wool shirt (L).

$16
Dacron-and-cotton shirt (N).

$170
Dyed cowhide jacket (I).

$38
Camel's-hair scarf (J).

$35
Wool trousers (K).

A casual wardrobe at this price level poses two questions—quality or quantity? It's still possible to combine the two and emerge with a good-looking, versatile group of wearables that cover a broad spectrum of your needs.

Far left: Layering shirt (L) with shirt (M), rounding off the look with trousers (G) and scarf (J). *Left:* Sweater (B), scarf (J), and trousers (K). *Above:* Sweater (F), shirt (N), and trousers (G). *Right:* A culling of the classics: jacket (I), shirt (N), and sweater (A) unite with trousers (K) to create a harmonious whole.

$ 700 DRESSY

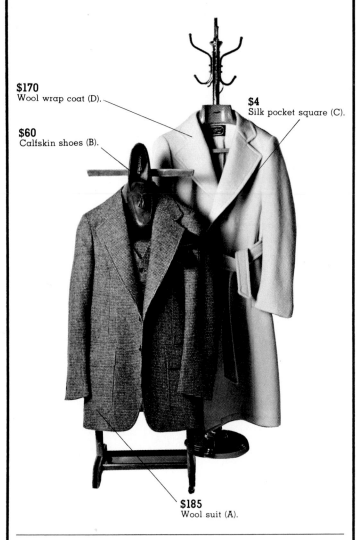

$170
Wool wrap coat (D).

$60
Calfskin shoes (B).

$4
Silk pocket square (C).

$185
Wool suit (A).

The work ethic applies to color and fabric too. When planning a business wardrobe at this or any price level, keep in mind the necessary harmonies. Simplicity is the route to authoritative elegance.

$20
Imported leather gloves (K).

$150
Wool-and-polyester suit with sweater vest (L).

$38
Acetate-and-nylon shirt (H).

$28
Cotton shirt (G).

$14
Wool cap (I).

$10
Silk tie (F).

$9
Polyester tie (E).

$12
Orlon acrylic sweater (J).

The maximum effect: suit (A), shirt (H), and tie (F).

Above: Suit trousers (A), sweater (J), shirt (H), silk square (C), gloves (K), cap (I), and coat (D) are brought together for a grand finale. *Below:* The outfit topped off with the coat (D), then rounded out with gloves (K) and shoes (B).

Sweater-vested
suit (L), shirt (G), and
tie (E) get together in
a very businesslike
way.

A neat reversal: suit jacket and sweater (L) combined with
suit trousers (A). Shirt (H) and pocket square (C), doubling as
a scarf, complete the image, with gloves (K) and cap (I).

$1,000 CASUAL

$100
Suede-and-leather crepe-soled shoes (G).

$110
Wool sweater (H).

$85
Wool gabardine trousers (I).

$60
Wool-and-acrylic trousers (J).

Luxury without a degree of constraint defeats its own purpose. With that in mind, a wardrobe at this price level should stress refinement of coloration and subtlety of cut more than the mere flashing of cash.

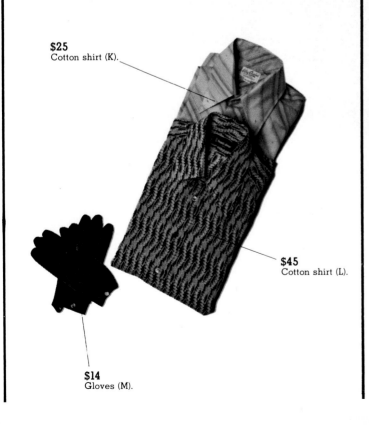

$25
Cotton shirt (K).

$45
Cotton shirt (L).

$14
Gloves (M).

$23
Scarf (B).

$16
Calfskin belt (E).

$65
Wool turtleneck (D).

$250
Suede-and-wool jacket (C).

$130
Polyurethane-protected cotton raincoat (A).

$76
Wool trousers (F).

The whole number: turtleneck (D) and jacket (C) blended with trousers (F), belt (E), and gloves (M).

The turtleneck (D) interlocks simply and beautifully with trousers (I).

Clothes that stay together play together: shirt (K), sweater (H), trousers (I), and shoes (G).

A more complex interpretation: shirt (K), sweater (H), scarf (B), and jacket (C).

For stormy
weather:
turtleneck (D)
and trousers (I)
are overlaid by
raincoat (A).

Applied logic:
shirt (L), scarf (B),
belt (E), and trou-
sers (J) sum up the
look.

$1,000 DRESSY

$28
Shetland sweater (C).

$55
Wool turtleneck (A).

$14
Acrylic sweater (B).

$200
Wool-and-polyester coat (D).

$10
Silk pocket square (F).

$250
Wool suit (E).

$95
Leather shoes (G).

$110
Wool sport coat (N).

$21
Leather gloves (P).

$50
Vest (O).

$38
Wool trousers (Q).

If anything, upper-level dressing should be flexible. After all, in buying the very best, you want the kind of wardrobe that's adaptable to any situation at virtually a moment's notice. A compact, rigorously chosen collection of clothes with an infinite capacity for modulation is what it's all about.

$35
Polyester-and-cotton shirt (J).

$18
Polyester-and-cotton shirt (I).

$28
Cotton shirt (H).

$18
Silk tie (M).

$18
Silk tie (K).

$11
Silk tie (L).

Left: A full-dress parade: sport coat (N), vest (O), shirt (I), tie (M), pocket square (F), and trousers (Q). *Right, top:* Easy dressing via sport coat (N), shirt (J), tie (L), pocket square (F), and suit trousers (E). *Right, center:* A quick match features sweater (C) and shirt (J). *Right, bottom:* A prepossessing combination offers suit jacket (E), shirt (J), sweater (C), pocket square (F)—used as a cravat—and trousers (Q). *Opposite page, top:* Coat (D) shares the billing with shirt (I), tie (M), gloves (P), trousers (Q), and shoes (G). *Opposite page, bottom:* Understated simplicity: sport coat (N), turtleneck (A), and pocket square (F).

How dressy can you get? Here, shirt (H), tie (K), suit (E), pocket square (F), and coat (D) are featured.

CHAPTER 6
CLOTHES CARE

Just because you've succeeded in stocking your closet and bureau drawers with an assortment of items that please you, combine nicely with one another, and send out the right combination of dots and dashes to satisfy your fashion Morse code, this doesn't mean that you don't have a thing to worry about. Now you've got to start thinking about how to keep your wardrobe in top condition and easily accessible. It's this element of planning that's critical these days when you pretty much have to do your own picking up after yourself. And besides, when you have to turn on a dime, in terms of time, you need crack organization.

Let's talk about fabric first. If we'd been writing this, say, seventy years ago, this would be an easier chapter to get through. Then, just before synthetics were invented, proceeding to transform everyone's way of life, we would have talked about essentially four types of fibers: cotton, wool, silk, and linen. All-natural (two of plant origin and two of animal), they kept our grandparents warm and in at least some cases chic. They are if anything more highly es-

teemed today than they were then, in part because of their increasing rarity.

There's a certain kind of man—you'll meet his ilk in trend-setting boutiques and older-fashioned department stores alike —who mourns the passing of the old fibers, by which he means the degree to which they've been supplanted by the synthetic ones in most people's wardrobes. And, he would add, even in the wardrobes of rich and conservative people who should know better and care more. Now, we're in sympathy with this person up to a point. We don't like double-knit suits that pill and bag at the knee, either. But we also have to admit that those four noble fabrics—wool, cotton, silk, and linen—are, if you're living on a budget, rather difficult to obtain.

Wool is warm (though it can be cool, too; the point is that it insulates you) and it holds a crease well, but you can't throw it in the washer and, even in this superscientific age, you still have to protect it against moths. Cotton is versatile, durable, and launders well. On the other hand, it's quick to wrinkle, can shrink (always unexpect-

NATURAL FIBERS

	COTTON	WOOL	SILK	LINEN
Characteristics	Despite the rise of synthetics, the world's major textile fiber. Durable, absorbent, resistant to shrinking, colorfast, washable. Wrinkles easily.	Soft, but with a lot of body, wool is the automatic choice of men everywhere whenever the weather turns cold. Strangely, it can also provide some insulation from heat. Holds a crease well.	The luxurious (and expensive) one. Dyes well, has good luster. Delicate but strong. Tricky to maintain; dry-cleaning or supercareful hand laundering recommended.	Cool and absorbent, formerly much prized as a summer-apparel staple. But wrinkles badly. Produced in limited quantities, and hence quite expensive.
Varieties	Batiste, broadcloth, chambray, chino, corduroy, denim, duck, flannel, gabardine (also wool), lawn, lisle, madras, muslin, oxford cloth, piqué, pongee, poplin, sailcloth, seersucker, shantung (also silk), terry cloth, twill (also wool), velour, velvet (also silk).	Cavalry twill, challis, flannel (also cotton), gabardine, melton, tweed. Also, such related specialty fibers as alpaca, camel's hair, cashmere, mohair, and vicuña, made from the hair of animals more or less sheeplike.	Brocade, chiffon, crêpe de chine, pongee, and shantung (both also cotton), satin, and velvet.	Cambric, damask, drill; jute a related fiber. Mostly the one word *linen* does it all.
Care	Hand launders easily without risk. If preshrunk it may be machine washed. Consult manufacturer's instructions. Iron with a hot iron if necessary. Dry-clean only "constructed" cotton garments.	Dry-clean virtually everything. Some items may be washed in special detergent like Woolite and usually by hand. Protect from moths.	In general, dry-clean. Occasionally, hand laundering in cool water is permissible. Avoid exposure to light over long periods, as it will discolor.	Wash or dry-clean, depending on complexity of garment's tailoring. Press with very hot iron.

General rules for hand washing woolens and silks, when this seems preferable to dry-cleaning: do not soak material, and use lukewarm, never hot, water. Use a mild (or, better yet, a special) soap. Squeeze the garment, never rub or twist it. Rinse gently but thoroughly. Squeeze dry; again, never twist. Roll the garment in a heavy towel and press out moisture with the hands. Lay it flat on more toweling and let it dry in a warm place but *not* near a direct source of heat. Never use a chlorine bleach on silk and wool. And never wash a garment that is "constructed"—that is, lined, padded, or otherwise intricately assembled from several different types and pieces of cloth.

edly, too) when washed, and—unless it's some subgenre like terrycloth—always requires ironing. Silk is beautiful, dyes with incredible conviction, and despite its delicacy is strong, but who can afford very much of it? And who wants to dry-clean his shirts all the time? Dry-cleaning may be fine for suits, but it never ever leaves a shirt feeling as clean or smelling as fresh as real soap-and-water laundering does. And linen, once the backbone of the summer-weight wardrobe because of its high moisture absorption and basic washability, wrinkles faster than you can get to the office.

In short, there's a place in this twentieth-century world, where foolproof personal services are getting harder and harder to find, for the fibers chemists have manufactured in laboratory test tubes and for the fabrics that have been woven from them (many of which, incidentally, are blends containing one or more of wool, cotton, silk, or linen). And there's likewise a place in your wardrobe for the clothing that results from these fabrics.

In general, man-made fibers don't begin to have the wear-and-maintenance problems of their natural counterparts. In addition, they cost less—often dramatically less. And each variety of fiber has its own special properties that allow it to do a particular job better and longer than anything else around. Since the commercial introduction of rayon in 1910 by the American Viscose Company, nineteen additional kinds of fiber have been invented. Nine of these —rayon, acetate, triacetate, acrylic, modacrylic, nylon, polyester, olefin, and spandex—form the backbone of the American apparel industry, accounting for fully 70 percent of all the raw fibers used by textile mills to produce woven and knitted fabrics.

Two subjects that warrant inclusion here are double-knits and permanent press. Neither describes a fiber of synthetic origin, but both have acquired related connotations.

Double-knit simply describes a firmly knit fabric that has two "right" sides, or faces, that can't be separated. Both sides may be plain, or one may have a contrasting pattern. The fabric is inherently stable, yet it "gives" to accommodate movement, snapping back into shape. A double-knit is usually made from polyester, either exclusively or in combination with another man-made fiber.

"Permanent press" refers to the finish applied to a fabric blend that usually contains polyester, nylon, or rayon. The fabric is treated with resins and then heat set, resulting in a garment that retains its original creases, pleats, and smooth appearance after laundering and machine drying. The finish is applied either at the mill, before delivery to the cutter, or after the garment has been cut, sewn, and pressed.

Now that you've familiarized yourself with the trinity of fiber, fabric, and finish, you can afford to approach your closet, swing open its door, and deal with the actual things you own. It goes without saying that you'll be keeping your clothes clean, but do you know how often and by what means; which garments should be hand washed, which dry-cleaned, and which can be safely thrown in the washing machine? Always consult the manufacturer's label now required by law to be stitched into all "major acquisition" garments, and honor its provisions.

Be especially careful of luxury items such as cashmere socks and sweaters and silk shirts, which should be treated as the indulgences they are. Although hand washing may be possible, it shouldn't be assumed that it is. Check with the store where you bought the item and if your salesperson doesn't seem to know the difference between cashmere and nylon, insist on speaking with the manager or buyer. (Of course, your dry cleaner will tell you that everything should be dry-cleaned; this is not necessarily the case.) And read through the following list to determine the best way of dealing with certain easily classified problem items.

BELTS

Leather and suede belts require the same care as shoes, which means occasional cleaning with saddle soap and waxing to keep them supple. The warping that may develop on the reverse side of a belt or at its seams from constant wear isn't necessarily bad; the belt is merely contouring itself to your body. When not being worn, belts should be hung by their buckles on a hook. This is preferable to rolling them in a drawer, since that can cause the ends to curl.

FOOTWEAR

Saddle soap is an excellent all-purpose cleaner for leather footwear of any color except white. It keeps shoes supple and removes surface dirt, but it does not impart a shine. Polish can be applied afterward, however, if you want to buff your shoes to a high gloss.

It's a good idea to polish new shoes before the first wearing to protect the surfaces from scuffing.

Patent leather shoes can be wiped clean with a damp cloth followed by a dry one, or you can use one of the commercially available patent leather polishes.

Suede shoes require the use of a stiff-bristled brush to loosen surface dirt and restore the original mat finish.

The best way to avoid breaking the backs of shoes is to slip into them with a shoehorn. After taking your shoes off, insert shoe trees to maintain their shape. Three types of shoe trees are available: wooden, which absorb moisture, and metal and plastic, which are lighter and ideal for traveling.

If you get caught in the rain, put trees in your shoes as soon as you remove them, and let them dry at room temperature. *Never* put them near a radiator; heat will cause the leather to dry out and crack. Suede shoes will require a light brushing once they're dry to bring up the nap.

Replace heels before they wear down completely or you'll ruin the shape of your shoes (not to mention throwing yourself off-balance).

Lastly, alternate your shoes, allowing for a day's rest between wearings, so that trapped moisture can evaporate thoroughly.

HOSIERY

Socks are probably the easiest items of apparel to care for. Those made of synthetic fibers can be machine washed in hot water and tumble dried. Wool or cotton socks should be washed in warm water and hung to dry to avoid shrinkage.

Although synthetic-fiber socks retain their shape well, they aren't as absorbent as those made of cotton or wool. So you might want to sprinkle foot powder inside your shoes to absorb the moisture away from your feet. This is especially important if you wear very thin socks.

JEWELRY

Jewelry should be kept in a special container with a soft lining to prevent scratching and other damage.

Silver and copper pieces require extra care to keep them tarnish-free. However, carefully read the instructions on all general-purpose metal cleaners and tarnish removers before purchasing; some warn against use with certain metals. Apply polish with a soft cloth to avoid scratching.

If possible, remove all jewelry before washing or bathing.

The brilliance of gemstones can be restored by gently washing them in a solution of ammonia and water or in any household window cleaner.

LEATHER

Suede and leather clothes should never be dry-cleaned. Find a reputable professional leather cleaner to whom you can entrust your garments. In addition, the continued use of leather-care products at home, such as the sprays that repel water, help to maintain a new look.

A suede garment can be spot-cleaned for a variety of stains (not including grease and perspiration, which result in discoloration) with the chemically treated sponge that usually comes with the item at the time of purchase. Suede, incidentally, has a distinct scent that may last for several months. As this scent can easily transfer itself to other clothes in your closet, it's wise to cover the suede item with a garment bag.

Smooth leathers can be wiped clean with a sponge dipped first in a mild solution of detergent and water and then in plain water. They should then be thoroughly dried with a soft cloth before storing.

All pieces of coordinated leather or suede outfits should be cleaned at the same time to avoid color variations. Furthermore, all leathers should be protected from overexposure to light and high temperatures. Finally, allow leather and suede to air out between wearings.

OUTERWEAR

To preserve its shape, a coat or jacket should always be hung on a wooden hanger, never on a hook. It should also be opened when you're sitting for any length of time to prevent undue stress on the fabric and structure.

Usually, outerwear will need cleaning only at the end of the season. It can then be stored in the protective cover the cleaner provides.

RAINWEAR

In general, dry cleaning is *not* recommended for rainwear because the solvents used in the process destroy the protective coatings usually applied to these garments. Rainwear with a polymer-based coating must be hand washed, whereas fabrics treated with a silicone-based substance *cannot* be washed in detergent, for the coating will dissolve. To remove surface dirt, simply wipe with a damp sponge or cloth.

Beyond washing, rainwear requires no special care. After coming in from a downpour, simply hang the coat on a wooden hanger (wire will cause rust stains) in a well-ventilated room to dry. Don't put a wet coat directly into a closet; it will develop a musty odor and may retain wrinkles.

SHIRTS

Although it's common practice to starch shirts to keep them wrinkle-free, the less starch used the better. The continual use of starch weakens the fabric and considerably shortens the life of a shirt. Permanent press shirts, of course, eliminate this problem, since they retain their shape regardless of how often they're washed.

If it's only the collar that concerns you, inserting stays in all of your shirts will keep the collars stiff and end the need for starch.

Launder shirts after each wearing, especially in summer, because body oils and grime easily become embedded in the collars and cuffs.

Shirts, because of their light weight, can be hung on wire hangers, but to prevent rust stains a cloth should be wrapped around the hanger first if the shirt is wet.

Be sure your underarm deodorant has dried before you slip into your shirt. The chemicals in these products can stain fabrics and cause them to deteriorate faster than usual.

When donning a tie, place it under the shirt collar and proceed to knot it rather than stand the collar up and then fold it over when the tie is secured. This enables the collar to retain its shape longer.

SUITS

Wishbone-shaped wooden hangers are the only proper ones for suits; they're contoured to fit jackets better than the wire models. So, switch over when your suits return from the cleaners.

When hanging a suit jacket, empty all the pockets and leave it unbuttoned to avoid straining the fabric. As for the trousers, again, empty the pockets, unzip the fly and remove the belt from the loops. If possible, don't stuff suits into an overcrowded closet. Ideally, there should be room for air to circulate around them.

It's a good practice not to wear the same suit two days in a row. During the rest period, the suit can spring back into shape.

Always dry-clean all the parts of a suit together—even if only one is soiled—to prevent mismatched pieces. Also, avoid overcleaning, which wears down the cloth.

SWEATERS

Machine or hand washing is safe for most knitted garments as long as you are following the care instructions on the labels. In most cases, however, machine driers should be avoided.

Wool and wool blends. Hand wash in cold water (hot water will shrink the yarn) and a special liquid cleaner such as Woolite. Rinse thoroughly in cold water and gently squeeze out excess water. Never wring or twist. To dry, lay the sweater on a towel atop a flat surface and smooth it out with your hand. Keep it away from heat.

Cotton and cotton blends. These tend to shrink less than wool. They can be machine washed in warm water, but not machine dried. Spread them on a towel to dry.

Synthetics. Most man-made fabrics can be safely machine laundered (warm water) and dried (low heat). However, some synthetics, like acrylic, should be air dried; others, like acetate, require dry-cleaning. Read the label for specifics.

Shake sweaters after wearing to allow the yarn to recoil. Fold with the sleeves tucked behind the body and the bottom under the top. (This method keeps the front flat and relatively wrinkle-free, even after packing.)

SWIMWEAR

Swimsuits should be washed in cold water and a mild detergent after each wearing to remove salt or chlorine. (Both are bleaching agents and will alter the color of the fabric if left in the suit.) Avoid hot water and machine drying, which cause shrinkage.

TIES

Hang ties on a special rack that can be installed on the inside of your closet door. Knitted ties, however, stretch out of shape easily; roll them and store in a drawer.

Don't put a tie away with the knot still in it. Untie it by reversing the knotting process. Loosening the knot and slipping the whole thing over your head puts unnecessary stress on the fabric.

Ties should be dry-cleaned and pressed. Follow the same rules as for any other item of apparel: avoid overcleaning and point out stains to the cleaner so he'll know how to treat them.

TROUSERS

Before hanging trousers, empty all pockets, unzip the fly, and remove the belt. These precautions will prevent them from losing their shape.

To avoid the crease that inevitably results from a crossbar hanger, invest in wooden clamp hangers that fasten onto the cuffs. The pants are hung straight with the two legs together, inseam to inseam.

Trousers are either washed or dry-cleaned, depending upon the fabric content. Read the label instructions.

UNDERWEAR

It's safe to machine wash undergarments; they can be either tumble dried or hung to dry. Cottons and blends should be washed in hot water and machine dried. Nylon fares best washed in warm water and dried on a low setting.

STAINS

The key thing to remember when dealing with stains is never to rub. You'll only succeed in removing the dye and possibly wearing a hole in the fabric itself. Stains on nonwashable materials are best treated by a good dry cleaner. Tell him exactly what caused the stain and what, if anything, you've already used on it. Then keep your fingers crossed.

Some more effective home remedies for stains include carbon tetrachloride (essentially lighter fluid), a solution of vinegar and water, even club soda. When using any liquid, dab it carefully on the stain with a clean white cloth. This will at least draw out surface dirt before it becomes embedded in the fabric. At the same time, have a piece of cloth (also, preferably, clean and white) underneath the stained portion of the garment to absorb any grime that's forced right through to the other side.

Don't forget about presoaks, especially the ones that contain enzymes, which really do help dislodge certain kinds of staining agents. Of course, the material in question must be washable. And don't forget, either, that housewife's favorite, good-old-fashioned bleach. Use it, however, only on white cotton or linen materials, never on colored ones and never under any circumstances on wool or silk, which it will proceed to gobble up.

Here are the specifics, in each case applicable only to washable garments unless otherwise stated.

Blood	Soak in lukewarm water and enzyme-containing presoak or detergent. Rinse well, then launder. On nonwashables, treat charily with a solution of cold water and table salt (two tablespoons per quart). Rinse equally carefully, then blot it with a towel.
Candle wax	Scrape off excess with a dull knife. Put the stained area between two absorbent surfaces (blotter paper will do, or clean cheesecloth) and press with a warm iron. If the stain remains, sponge it with carbon tetrachloride.
Chewing gum	Scrape off the excess with a dull knife. Sponge it with carbon tetrachloride.
Coffee and chocolate	Soak in warm water with an enzyme-containing product. Launder.
Grass	Rub with suds (or soak in the enzyme-containing product mentioned above). If the stain remains, use chlorine bleach (but note the earlier precaution).
Grease and tar	Place a towel under the stain. Use ample cleaning fluid (carbon tetrachloride). Launder to remove the ring and smell.
Lipstick	Sponge with carbon tetrachloride. If the stain remains, use chlorine bleach (again noting precaution).
Mildew	Launder with detergent and chlorine bleach (using the latter if color and fabric permit).
Perspiration	Launder with detergent in hot water. Bleach if necessary and feasible. If fabric is nonwashable but still colorfast, try sponging with water.

INDUSTRIAL CHIC

Containers of industrial design are the newest and most creative solution going to the problem of organizing your clothes and other belongings. Neat, practical, and very efficient, they can instantly give you a place for just about everything you own.

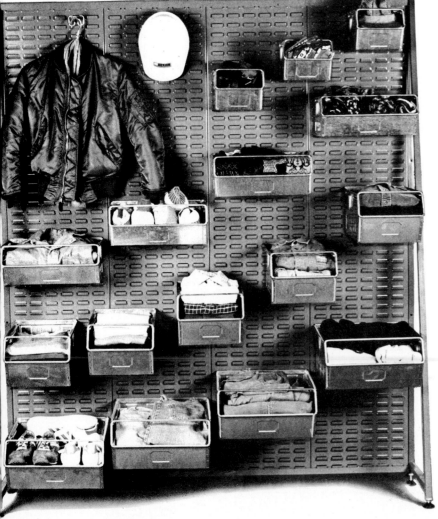

Far left, top: **This efficient clothes system from Sweden has a metal frame on which plastic-coated baskets are hung.** *Far left, bottom:* **Originally designed for automotive parts, this system begins with a metal framework, available in various sizes. Steel tote bins are then clipped on in any quantity.** *Left, top:* **This cub-style clothes bin comes in red, brown, white, or black.** *Left, bottom:* **Shirts and shoes are neatly organized in this container.** *Above:* **Plenty of deep storage space is afforded in this filing system.**

When clothes are clean and stain- and wrinkle-free, one still can't rest easy. Clothes have to be accessible, too, organized in such a way that they're minimally space consuming and maximally visible. Closets and bureau drawers are your traditional allies here, and they're good ones. Drawers pull out, allowing you to scan their contents, then they close up again, keeping things out of the light (which fades them) and the dust (which soils and dulls them). Closets afford a place to hang things and generally have a few shelves for good measure. Their floors are places to put shoes and even trunks, which can take up the slack your bureau drawers leave. The chances are you can do just fine with what you have already—if only you'll cull out the unwearable clothes of half a lifetime and throw or give them away, leaving breathing space for the ones that really matter and the newcomers that provide any wardrobe with joie de vivre and a reason to go on. Now reorganize, putting glove with glove, not only right hand with left, but pair with pair. And include mittens, too. This way, shelf by shelf, your available space will assume a shape and a logic, the combination of which will allow you to lay hands on things, even traditionally hard-to-locate things like gloves, in no time flat.

And if you're really interested in a change, in the cross of compartmentalization with the twentieth century, in a radical solution to an ancient problem, consider some of the containers now available, virtually all of industrial origin and many surprisingly cheap. Why not welcome at least one version of the future into your dressing room? You'll find yourself in possession of both an organizational note and a design aesthetic.

CHAPTER 7
KEEPING FIT

DIET

Clothes don't really make the man, they simply cover up for him. Underneath it all, there's still the same old body with the familiar imperfections to deal with. All of us are willing to concede that fitness is a good thing; the question is how to achieve it. This chapter guides you through some of the intricacies of pulling your body together not only in terms of physical exertion but also in some of the subtler ways, the massages and diets, for instance, that will put you in top condition and ensure that you stay there.

Let's start with the true building blocks of a better body. Good nutrition is the cornerstone of muscle tone, so if you start an exercise program before correcting diet deficiencies, you're putting the cart before the horse. The difference food can make in providing the power to see you through an exercise program is dramatic. Indications of an inadequate diet include extreme tiredness after climbing a flight of stairs, an inclination to sleep more than average, sluggishness, and laziness. If your body isn't receiving enough food, especially pro-

tein, it will destroy its own cells for food, hence your exhaustion. Your appearance will also reflect this decay. Fortunately, the body begins rebuilding itself upon receiving an improved diet, so all is not lost.

What comprises a balanced meal? Carbohydrates for fast energy, fats for long-term energy, proteins for cell building. These three nutrients must be obtained at the same time to be fully effective. Eating carbohydrates alone, for example, creates an imbalance in your system, providing a rush of energy that soon fizzles out. Do this often enough and you'll damage your health.

If you have a special problem, such as obesity, you can cut down on carbohydrates by utilizing the energy stored in your body as fats. In any event, protein intake must be kept up, especially if you're very thin. You should also be aware of your cholesterol level, unless you're involved in a regular, strenuous exercise program. Physical activity does work against cholesterol build-up, but a light exercise program may not ensure this.

Protein is the specific nutrient needed to build and maintain muscles and muscle tone. No serious athlete would consider a training program without consuming adequate amounts of protein. Weightlifters are especially aware of the importance of these amino acids; thus they take protein supplements. The Food and Nutrition Board of the National Research Council maintains that a 150-pound male requires 56 grams of protein a day (the amount contained in about a half pound of chicken), taken in doses of approximately 20 grams per meal. It also points out, however, that since the body assimilates only about 75 percent of the food eaten, more than the Recommended Daily Allowance should be taken.

To compute your approximate RDA, divide your body weight by two and subtract 20 from the quotient. For example, if you weigh 175 pounds, your daily requirement is 68 grams of protein.

Almost as necessary as food to a successful shaping up program, vitamin pills, containing balanced amounts of vitamins, minerals, and trace elements, provide many of the micronutrients your diet may lack. According to the Vitamin Information Service of Hoffman LaRoche, Inc., 20 to 50 percent of all Americans risk not getting enough vitamins, through improper diet or neglect. If you're adding the stress of regular, thrice-weekly workouts, make certain that your vitamin intake at least matches the U.S. Recommended Daily Allowance.

Smoking lowers the level of vitamin C in your system. Alcohol interferes with the body's utilization of thiamine (B1), riboflavin (B2), and folic acid. The minerals iron and calcium are also likely to be deficient in the diet of many Americans. Certain food processes, such as freezing, pasteurization, and long-term storage, can also affect the vitamin content in foods.

Vitamin C is a necessary micronutrient for the person who exercises. It helps to build strong body cells and blood vessels and to hold cell walls together. Biotin (vitamin H) aids in the immediate metabolism of carbohydrates, fats, and proteins, which is especially important for athletes, who eat more than the average person. Vitamin B5 (pantothenic acid) also helps with the breakdown of foods. B2 is essential for healthy skin.

Vitamins can be taken at any time; it's not necessary to include them with meals, but neither is it advisable to pour them into an empty stomach. You might find it best to take them with milk or yogurt or after meals.

In the United States, Recommended Daily Allowances—supplanting the former Minimum Daily Requirements—have been established for twelve essential vitamins. There are other essential vitamins, but no RDA has yet been set.

VITAMIN	RDA
A	5,000 International Units (IU)
B1	1.5 milligrams (mgs)
B2	1.7 mgs
B3 (niacin)	20 mgs
B5 (pantothenic acid)	10 mgs
B6 (pyridoxine)	2 mgs
B12 (cyanocobalamin)	6 micrograms (mcgs)
Bc (folic acid)	0.4 mgs
C (ascorbic acid)	60 mgs
D	400 IU
E	30 IU
H (biotin)	0.3 mgs

If you don't want to sit around contemplating the protein content of a chicken leg, certain books can guide you. The classic is Adelle Davis's *Let's Eat Right To Keep Fit*, which includes an extensive list of protein contents in common foods. *The Barbara Kraus Dictionary of Protein* gives the protein content of almost everything.

Eat three meals a day, concentrating on protein. The average man should have twenty grams of protein or the equivalent of three eggs (not fried) for breakfast. You'll be surprised how this protein eases the craving to eat something again before lunchtime. For lunch or dinner, eat lean meat or fish with whatever nonfattening foods you like. Foods always to avoid are prepared breakfast cereals, bread, pastas, sweet wines, liqueurs, beer, jellies, jams, preserves, ice cream, cakes and candies, sugar, chestnuts, apricots, dates, bananas, potatoes, fats, duck, spare ribs, sausages, bacon, luncheon meats, whole milk, deep-fried snacks, and puddings.

Three final pointers. Remember that unsweetened grapefruit juice or quinine water before eating tends to dull the appetite if you're watching your weight. Excessive use of salt leads to water retention (weight), so use it sparingly. And finally, never undertake a weight-reduction program of any kind without consulting your doctor.

Here follow three classic diets. Choose the one that fits your temperament and psychological needs.

WEIGHT WATCHERS DIET

Source. Based on a diet developed by Dr. Morton Glenn, director of the Obesity Clinic of the New York City Department of Health, and popularized by Jean Nidetch, beginning in 1963.

Method. Select foods from various categories—in carefully measured quantities—while adhering to weekly allotments. Dieter must eat *everything* on his menu and have three meals a day. The Weight Watchers diet has recently been revised to include small portions of starches and fats on a daily basis.

How it works. The unique aspect of Weight Watchers is its supportive psychological group-therapy approach to weight loss. Weekly meetings with a leader chart progress and discuss problems. The diet itself is basically a well-rounded, nutritionally sound plan that combines caloric reduction in food intake with high-protein, low-fat foods. Starches are moderately used.

Reduction rate. A progressive weight loss of two pounds a week is about average.

Mandatory foods. Fish at least five times a week; liver at least once a week; fruits, three a day; unlimited amounts of such vegetables as celery, lettuce, watercress, radishes, and moderate amounts of other vegetables; eggs, no more than four a week; bread, two slices a day; and skim milk, two glasses a day.

SAMPLE DIET MENU
Breakfast
½ cup orange juice
Poached egg on toast
Diet margarine
Coffee or one glass skim milk
Lunch
4 oz. tuna fish
½ tbsp. mayonnaise
String beans
Watercress
1 slice bread
Beverage
Dinner
6 oz. roast beef
Brussels sprouts
Summer squash
Celery hearts
Diet margarine
Beverage

Foods not allowed. Pizza, peanuts, ketchup, sweets of any kind, sardines, soups, bacon, beer, and booze.

Advantages. The diet allows for the psychological need to eat and, through the group approach, becomes mandatory to follow. There's also plenty of variety.

Disadvantages. For some, the careful measuring of food and of weekly allotments within food categories can be confusing.

LOW-CARBOHYDRATE DIET

Source. *The Drinking Man's Diet Cookbook*, edited by Robert W. Cameron.

Method. Limit your daily intake of carbohydrates to sixty grams, making meat, fish, poultry, and eggs the backbone of your diet. Familiarize yourself with the carbohydrate content of common foods and stay away from those with a high count. Fruits, surprisingly, are high in carbohydrates, so go easy on them. Starches and cereals, of course, are high in both calories and carbohydrates. A piece of plain fudge or of iced layer cake can take you right up to your daily quota.

How it works. As in any diet where carbohydrate restrictions go below the amount

SAMPLE DIET MENU
Breakfast
½ cup strawberries with cream
2 soft-boiled eggs
1 thin slice buttered toast
Lunch
Broiled chopped beef
Sliced tomato-and-cucumber salad
Dinner
Chicken breast à la Suisse
Broccoli with almonds and butter
Green salad with plain dressing
Wedge of cheese
Small bunch of grapes

usually taken in, the body reacts by burning its own fat reserves.

Reduction rate. A couple of pounds a week is the bet, with a possible fourteen-pound loss in the first month.

Foods allowed. Lean meats, fish, and poultry, eggs, mayonnaise, butter, salad oils, avocados, almost all cheeses, coffee with cream and, of course, booze.

Foods not allowed. Ice cream, cakes, pies, condensed milk, peanuts, pistachio nuts, dried coconut, figs and dates, prunes, beans, pasta, beer, sweet wines and soft drinks.

Advantages. The diet is relatively easy to follow and doesn't involve careful measuring of food intake. It's easy to remain with while dining out. There's no psychological depression.

Disadvantages. Some adherents experience sugar cravings. A drastic cutback of carbohydrate ingestion can lead to nervousness and fatigue, so you shouldn't go under the sixty-gram-a-day allotment.

DR. ATKINS' SUPERDIET

Source. *Dr. Atkins' Diet Revolution: The High Calorie Way to Stay Thin Forever* by Robert Atkins, M.D.

Method. Pick menu from a list of permitted foods—low in carbohydrates, high in protein. Eat until you're full, but don't eat if you're not hungry. There's also a graduated increase in the variety of foods permitted. After the first twelve days of the diet, you may add fruit and a glass of wine or 2 ounces of vodka, gin, or whiskey.

How it works. Dr. Robert Atkins feels that high sugar consumption is the bugaboo of American obesity. High sugar consumption can cause hypoglycemia (low blood sugar), which in turn produces a vicious circle of high sugar (pure carbohydrate) consumption. This diet works by completely eliminating starches and sugars, including instead meats, vegetables, judicious amounts and varieties of both fruits and dairy products, plus "megadoses" of vitamins. The diet is a calorically unrestricted low-carbohydrate regimen that causes the body to burn its excess fats because insufficient carbohydrates are eaten.

Reduction rate. A steady three to four pounds a week. (Dr. Atkins himself claims to have lost twenty-five pounds in six weeks!)

Foods allowed. Meats of all kinds, in any quantity, except with fillers (like meatballs); vegetables of all kinds; fish and poultry; sour cream, butter, and mayonnaise—in judicious amounts; and wine or liquor in moderation.

Foods not allowed. Sugar (except artificial sweetener), rice, potatoes, bread,

SAMPLE DIET MENU
Breakfast
Cheddar cheese omelet
Black coffee
Lunch
Chef salad with turkey, chicken, lean ham, cherry tomatoes and mixed greens
Dinner
Shrimp cocktail with horseradish
Asparagus with a dollop of hollandaise
Endive salad
Coffee
Dr. Atkins' cheesecake
1 glass dry red wine

pasta, peanuts, cashews, chestnuts and chewing gum.

Advantages. Dieter experiences lack of hunger along with a remarkable upsurge of energy. Depression is kept to a minimum, as is the urge to cheat, due to the variety of food.

Disadvantages. Some dieters experience sugar cravings. Certain doctors feel that severely limiting one's carbohydrate intake can harm brain and nerve cells; others believe the high intake of cholesterol may lead to heart disease. A controversy has erupted among medical people concerning this diet, partly because Dr. Atkins' book is critical of them and partly because his diet strongly veers from contemporary thinking on weight reduction.

SHAPING UP

With your nutritional restructuring program in the works, it's time to turn to externals, your physical dimensions and what to do about them. There are numerous ways to put muscles on your frame and achieve anything from Arnold Schwarzenegger's flashing steel plates to the lean toughness of Paul Newman to the ugly-but-strong Soviet Olympic team look. Since the bookstores are flooded with literature, we won't detail all the methods here but will offer some pointers to get you started.

The most important factor in shaping up is not the exercises you do but how you do them. If you have a basic mental antipathy toward the workout, you probably won't see much change in your physique. You must start with and maintain a positive attitude. If you don't enjoy your exercise program, find another that's more fun. "Purpose" exercises, such as gymnastics and dance, or supervised systems, such as Bodyworks and the Nickolaus Technique, may be effective. In the gym a buddy will keep your spirits up. If you don't like the gymnasium atmosphere, finding it intimidating or boring, your regimen there probably won't prove very effective. Examine your attitude toward a health club before signing up.

Josef Rottenburger, a New York masseur, Olympic athlete (1936), and strong-as-a-bull septuagenarian, keeps some of the world's most famous bodies in shape with massage and exercise. Rottenburger points out that the exercises you do should depend upon your age and your body's flexibility.

The following exercises, he feels, are best for developing suppleness.

A "big belly." The sit-up is still the best exercise. Keep legs extended and feet braced while doing them. Afterward, try this: make circular motions with arms and legs. Then raise arms and legs and rotate them first in one direction, then the other.

Legs. For flexibility and strength, lie on your back. Extend toes into a point toward the floor. Then pull toes back so heels extend as far forward as possible. Turn over onto stomach. Grasp ankles and kick butt with heels, alternating them.

Pectorals and arms. Pushups.

Hips and waist. Stand with feet apart, arms extended upward. Rotate upper torso on hips. Next, bend to one side, then the other. Then brace hands at small of back and arch spine and neck backward. Place hands on neck and bend forward to knees. Straighten up. Do this once.

The other exercises should be repeated according to your ability. "Never overdo," Rottenburger advises. "About eight to ten movements done three times a week should be enough. Work straight through; don't rest between exercises."

WEIGHT-LIFTING

If you either don't like gyms or don't live near one, you can still work out with weights. For about the cost of a year's membership in a health club—or even less—you can equip yourself with a rea-

WEIGHT TRAINING

Steve Laitman of the Profile Health Club, New York City, a weight lifter and health club owner, has worked with Dan Lurie, one of the stars of the weight-lifting world, and is the holder of several weight-lifting titles himself. His philosophy of shaping up includes, first of all, enjoying the exercises. He feels that you minimize the benefits if you're mentally fighting the work. While working out, he suggests performing the entire regimen in a strict, continuous fashion, with very little rest between exercises. "This provides cardiovascular benefits as well as cosmetic." Do no more than a half-hour of exercise at any time, he advises, and work out three times a week.

STOMACH SQUEEZES
1. Lie flat on your back, with knees in the air.
2. Do a one-inch sit-up, squeezing the stomach muscles at the same time. Do as many as possible.

Squeezes are better than sit-ups, according to Laitman, because they don't strain the lower back.

2

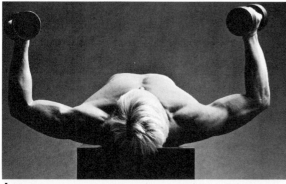

1

2

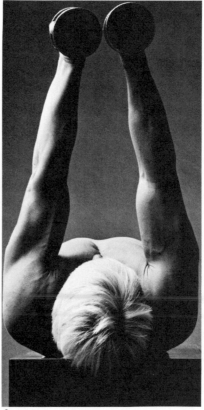

3

BENT-ARM FLIES
(for the pectoral muscles)

1. Lie flat on the floor or on a bench, holding a dumbbell in each hand, arms bent.
2. Bring dumbbells straight up over your chest at an even pace. 3. Touch the dumbbells together directly over your chest, then return to starting position.

Repeat ten to twelve times with weights you can handle comfortably. Increase repetitions as your chest strengthens.

STANDING BARBELL CURLS
(for the arms)

1. Stand holding barbell of comfortable weight as pictured. 2. Bring barbell up toward chest, keeping the bar straight. 3. Complete the movement as close to chest as possible. Lower barbell to starting position.

Repeat ten to twelve times at beginning. Increase repetitions as you see fit.

1

2

3

1

2

3

DEEP-KNEE BENDS
(for the thighs)

1. Stand with back as straight as possible and heels raised—preferably on a two-by-four-inch board—to take strain off lower back. Use a lightweight barbell resting comfortably on shoulders. 2. Keeping back straight, slowly lower yourself to a squatting position. 3. Complete the movement as shown, or as close as possible, then stand up again.

Repeat twenty to thirty times, if you can without fatigue.

PULLOVERS
(for raising rib cage)

1. Use either a single dumbbell, as pictured, or a lightweight barbell. Start with weight held over chest. 2. Lower the weight slowly back over your head. With full control (meaning don't drop it), lower the weight to a comfortable point above your head.

Be careful not to use too heavy a weight and not to strain your arms. Repeat movement ten to twelve times at beginning.

1

2

CALISTHENICS

Jack LaLanne is best known for his TV shows on which he takes his viewers through a systematic routine of exercises. During his career (he's now sixty-two), he swam from Alcatraz to Fisherman's Wharf wearing handcuffs, towed a twenty-five-hundred-pound cabin cruiser through the Golden Gate Channel, and has continually given active support to the President's Council on Physical Fitness. Jack LaLanne Health Spas, of course, dot the nation, and recently he wrote a book, *For Men Only*, with Jim Allen, setting forth his fitness plan for men. The book, as well as other Jack LaLanne products and catalogs are available from The Jack LaLanne Company, 621 Allen Avenue, Glendale, Calif. 91201.

The regimen shown here—demonstrated by LaLanne himself—is for the man who has already been doing exercises, rather than the untrained beginner. Gauge the repetitions of each exercise to your own strength.

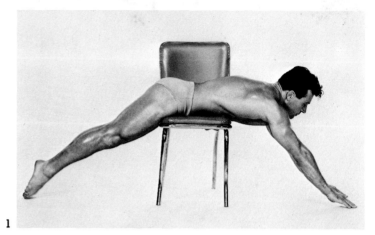

1

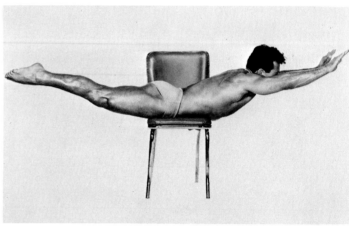

2

THE LEGS SPLIT
(for thighs and hips)

Start from standing position (not shown), hands on hips. 1. Lunge forward on left leg, extending right leg to rear. 2. Reverse; lunge forward on right leg, extending left leg to rear and immediately return to standing position.

To receive maximum benefit you must split as low as possible.

THE ARCH ON CHAIR
(for the lower back)

1. Assume position shown on chair, arms and legs rigid. 2. Arch back by lifting arms and legs, then return to first position.

Keep arms and legs rigid at all times.

1

2

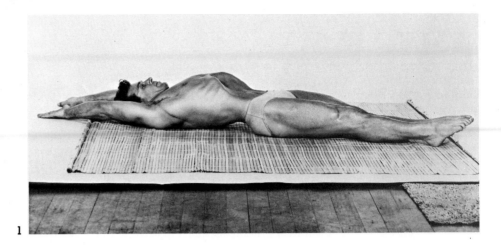

1

THE JACKKNIFE
(for stomach and entire body)

A very advanced exercise, not for the beginner. 1. Lie flat on back, legs extended, toes pointed, arms stretched above head. 2. Bringing legs up as shown, quickly touch toes with hands.

2

1

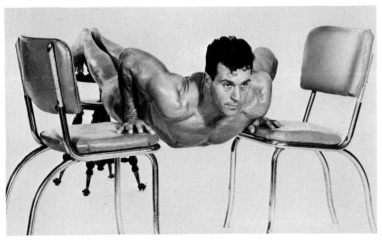

2

THE PUSHUP
(for chest and triceps)

This can be done on the floor, but the drop between the chairs gives more stretch to the muscles. 1. Take position shown on chairs, body and arms rigid. 2. Bend arms; lower body as shown. Immediately straighten arms and return to first position.

Note: Keep body rigid at all times. Keep hands a few inches farther apart than width of shoulders.

GYMNASTICS

Ed Gagnier is head gymnastics coach at Iowa State University, Ames, and a member of the Olympic Committee. His gymnastics team was the N.C.A.A. Champion in 1971, 1973, and 1974. Gagnier was a member of the Olympics team in 1956.

Gagnier provides a series of gymnastics movements which can be used for general fitness and body development. They comprise a regimen for someone who likes this type of exercise but isn't planning on becoming a champion gymnast. He suggests repeating each complete movement five times, holding the last position about three seconds each time. Because gymnastics develop the entire body, not just particular muscles, we aren't specifying parts of the body in this section. Is there an age limit for beginning these exercises? Gagnier feels any healthy man up to about age forty-five can begin this regimen. He notes, too, that a teacher is necessary to learn the correct way of doing these movements.

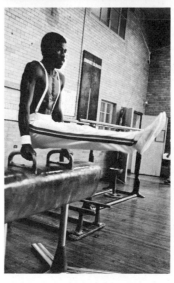
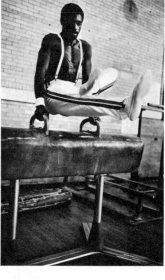

VAULTING
Squat up onto the "horse," as shown, and hop off. An advanced movement would be to go right over the "horse" without stopping, knees bent in close to the body (not shown).

L-HOLD
Sit in middle of "horse," both hands on the pommel. Raise up, legs straight out. If you cross one foot over the other knee, it brings the weight closer to the hips (as shown in last picture) and makes it easier to perform at the beginning stages. Hold the last position three seconds.

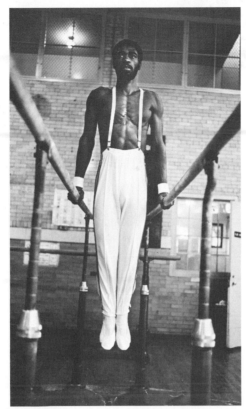

STILL DIP
On parallel bars, hang with arms bent; straighten up. Hold for three seconds. An advanced variation of this (not shown) would be a "Swinging Dip," done with feet behind and brought forward on completion of the movement.

SKIN THE CAT
Total movement: hold rings; bend arms and legs; go all the way over, tuck legs, and hang; then tuck legs up and return the same way. Bending of arms is permissible and a three-second hold isn't necessary.

sonably adequate body-building setup at home. Here's what you'll need to start:

Barbell *(about $17)*. This is the bar on which you hang the weights and is the most important single purchase you'll make. It's about 5½ feet long and has two stabilizers to keep the weights steady. It can be used by itself for beginning lifts and warm-ups or for calisthenics. Its fifteen-pound weight must be included when you're judging how much to lift.

Weights *(about 50 cents per pound)*. At the start, equip yourself with about one hundred pounds of weights in varying sizes: five-pound, ten-pound, twenty-pound. Weights, plus the barbell, should provide enough equipment to start an effective program.

Bench press *(about $65)*. This becomes necessary when the weights become too heavy to heave onto your chest for certain important exercises. It's a padded metal bench with a weight stand attached to one end.

Dumbbells *(about $10 a pair)*. You won't need these at the beginning. Any exercises that call for dumbbells can be done by using loose weights. Later, if you want to refine your developed muscles, you can invest in these.

John C. Grimek has been working out for some fifty years. He also writes and edits for *Muscular Development* magazine. His approach to weightlifting is sensible and knowledgeable, so we asked him to advise the beginner.

Grimek recommends starting out lightly. Determine how much weight you can comfortably lift ten to twelve times. You may want to start with a total of 25 pounds, including the barbell. "The fact that you're doing the exercise correctly is more important than how much you lift."

How often? Three times a week or every other day. "However, you may want to rest for two days in the beginning, if you're really tired. Body and muscles should have a day of rest after a workout, especially with novices."

How many reps? "This depends upon your strength. It's best not to push past your limit. Do about 10 or 12 repetitions at the beginning and increase the number when they become effortless."

What about soreness? "If a person works out progressively, he should experience little soreness. If you do feel sore, do a little follow-up exercise to circulate fresh blood and flush out toxins."

What if you stop? "First, cut calories down. This will prevent the muscles you've developed from turning to fat. Once you're in shape, you can stay that way by watching yourself. After you've trained for years, you won't have to work out religiously; periodic workouts will be enough to preserve your build."

What about going back after you stop? "You can revive the strength you had, but your coordination will be affected. You may be clumsy in performing the exercises, although you will have no problem lifting the weights."

General advice. "A person should feel comfortably tired immediately after a workout, but after a shower, he should feel more energetic than before. If you are still tired, you're doing too damn much."

If you plan to work out with weights at home, arm yourself ahead of time with books on the subject as a kind of preview. Bookstores aren't likely to carry them, but they're available wherever weights are sold. Bob Hoffman has written a series of books on workouts with and without weights (Strength and Health Publishing Co., 2652 North Ridge Avenue, York, Pa. 17403). Joe Weider (Weider Health and Fitness, 21100 Erwin Street, Woodland Hills, Calif. 91364) offers a complete training manual for $10. The Joe Bonomo Culture Institute (1841 Broadway, New York, N.Y. 10023), publishes the handiest and least expensive books (about 35 cents each, in some cases). *Weightlifting and Weight Training* by George W. Kirkley (Arco, $1.25) is available in bookstores.

AEROBICS

Proper muscle tone involves not only the suppleness and elasticity of individual muscles but also the proper functioning of your respiratory and cardiovascular systems. Massage, believe it or not, can help you achieve this, as can simple proper breathing, but even more to the point is the range of exercises that take their name from the fact that they eat up oxygen. We're talking, of course, of *aerobic* exercises.

Neither weight-lifting nor spot exercises, you see, does a thing for one of your body's most important muscles—the heart. You may be making that body irresistible and strong, but you're treating it as a mere container, and you're in no way ensuring the longevity of its contents. So consider a *combination* of exercise regimens, at least one of which has a pronounced aerobic component that will have you breathing fast and deep. Jogging, swimming, and cycling are good—and fairly standard, equipment-free—aerobics; tennis and skiing also fit into this broad category. All will trim you down by toning, rather than inflating, muscles. Perhaps more important, they'll increase your blood circulation, which is the basic aim of any exercise program and a cornerstone of cardiovascular health.

Perhaps most gratifying, you'll find that the amount of energy regularly available to you (when you get up in the morning, for instance, or in the late afternoon) increases dramatically. Of course, your workouts will have to be regular (three or four times a week is recommended), intense (if you don't sweat and occasionally run out of breath, you're not being hard enough on yourself), and of at least forty-five minutes' duration before any such benefits will be derived. In the meantime, here are a few tips to get you going:

Swimming. Swimming is considered to be one of the best all-around strenuous exercises (walking is the best nonstrenuous).

This is because it combines deep breathing, energetic pumping of the heart to increase circulation, maximum stretching and contracting of the muscles, and the whittling away of fatty tissue. The only problem: you need a body of water.

Breathing exercises. Deep breathing is the most important factor in all exercise programs. Too many people hold their breath while working out, thus reducing the effects of the exercise. Breathing keeps your energy up and renews and refreshes your system. In fact, you could conceivably stay in shape just by mastering a series of breathing techniques.

This breathing exercise will help to relax and tone your entire body:

1. Stand erect, hands at sides, feet together or close enough to allow for standing on toes without teetering.

2. Inhale deeply and completely fill lungs, pulling in stomach muscles and raising arms slowly. The arms should be tensing isometrically and the hands clenching into fists.

3. At the same time, slowly clench buttocks and raise yourself onto your toes.

4. Slowly exhale, returning to original stance. Relax.

Initially, do this exercise ten to fifteen times each day. However, make sure that your stomach muscles have completely relaxed at the end of each exhalation.

MASSAGE

"In Europe, all athletes have masseurs," says Pablo Fraenkel, one of New York's leading masseurs. "Here, it's mostly boxers who incorporate massage into their training." Massage helps athletes to warm up; it loosens and relaxes the muscles and balances the body and mind. Tension interferes with coordination—which is very important to shaping up. To perform exercises correctly, your body must be at your mind's command. "When you're tense you don't

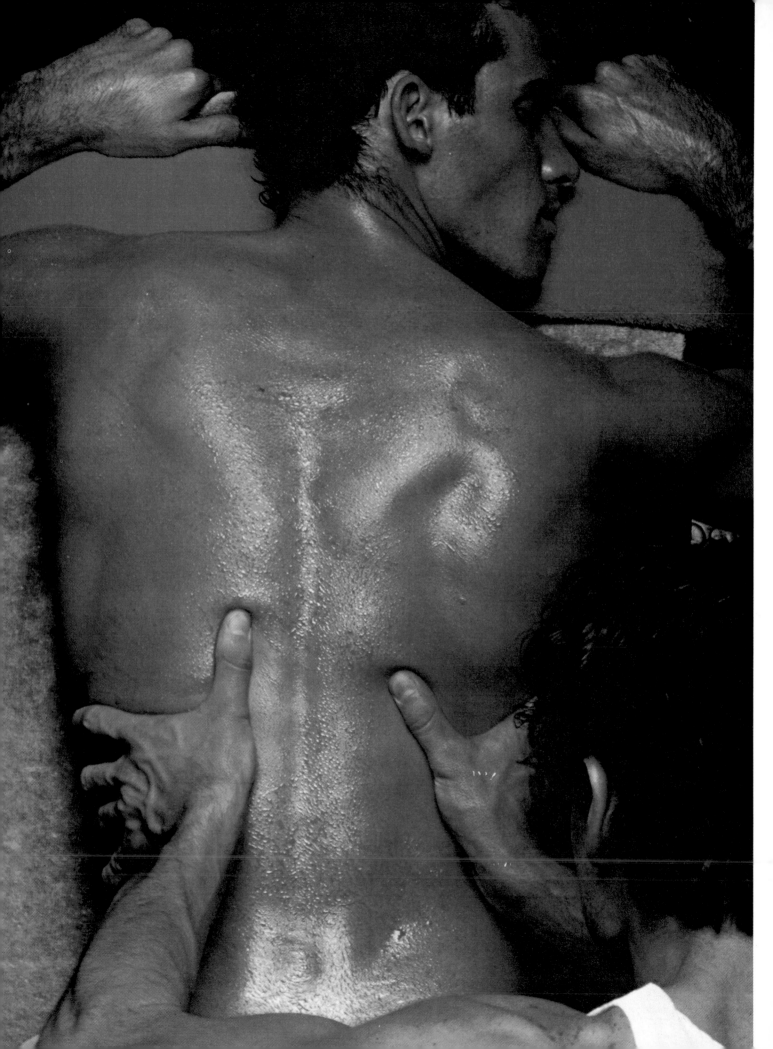

respond quickly from thought to action," Fraenkel adds. He also makes these points:

☐ After strenuous physical exercise, the resultant chemical changes cause an increase of toxins in the body. A massage after a workout circulates the blood and helps to expel toxins.

☐ A massage helps your body to utilize nutrients more effectively. Less food turns to fat. The result is increased energy and a more efficient shaping up.

☐ Massage can help relieve postexercise soreness as a result of strained muscles.

Different strokes. Several types of massage are available in the United States. Since many practitioners don't make their living from massage, the best way to find a good masseur is by asking around. Here's what you'll be looking for.

Swedish massage. It's been said that Swedish, French, and German massages are all the same. The different designations merely indicate where in Europe a masseur learned his technique. A European massage is comprised of five basic hand movements on the body. Effleurage is a firm, smooth, upward stroking along the body to increase circulation of blood and lymph fluids to the heart. Petrissage, a grasping, kneading movement on the muscles, reaches deeper than effleurage. This picking up and grasping relaxes tension knots and breaks up muscular adhesions. Tapotement is a firm, but not hard, hacking, chopping motion with cupped hands or the sides of the hands. It aids general relaxation and drives away tension with its steady beat-beat-beat. Vibration is gentle pressing with the fingertips while vibrating the hand. It's primarily used on extra-sensitive areas such as the face which shouldn't be massaged too strongly. Friction is movement of the joints. All these motions are used as needed during the course of a massage to achieve the desired effect.

Shiatsu. This is a very strong method of massage, often called acupressure. It involves the use of the acupuncture points on the body to release blocked energies causing discomfort. By exerting deep pressure on specific areas of the body, the shiatsu masseur can release tensions, allow the energies to flow again through the body, and induce relaxation.

Reflexology, also called zone therapy, involves massage and pressure on certain points of the feet to achieve release in other parts of the body. Stomach problems, for instance, require applying pressure to points on the soles of the feet to allow blocked energies to flow freely. There's a pressure point somewhere on the soles of the feet for every part of the body.

Oriental massage. This broad categorization covers a multitude of massage techniques, each designed to cope with some problem of the body. Basically, oriental massage is comprised of sixty-four different movements, which the skilled masseur brings into play as needed. They can be as simple as pressure applied to a muscle or as complex as a masseur walking on his client's back or lifting him onto his own back as a means of stretching muscles. Although some of the movements are strong enough to be painful, the techniques don't cause discomfort, as the body is brought into a healthy state. It's said that if a massage technique hurts, that technique is needed. No massage, properly performed, causes pain to a healthy body.

Neck massage. Unfortunately, most masseurs neglect or minimalize treatment of the neck, shoulders, and scalp. Tension usually manifests itself at the base of the skull, producing pain, tension knots, and scalp or shoulder tightness as the pain and tension feed on each other. Tense necks cause most headaches. Even the discomfort of sinus headaches can be relieved by massaging the back of the neck. When properly given, the client is sitting in a chair or on a table and the masseur stands behind him, working on the neck and carefully supporting the head. The shoulders and scalp, as well as the forehead, temples, and sides of the face, may be treated. A successful neck massage brings quick relief from tension and pain.

CHAPTER 8
GROOMING

The American man has always been encouraged to spend as much time and energy cultivating his musculature as he saw fit. But it's only within the last ten years or so that he's gotten society's go-ahead to focus comparable attention on above-the-neckline matters without having to worry about being labeled a narcissist or a fop. And what a ten years it has been, for him and for an ever-increasing army of hairstylists and cosmetics and fragrance manufacturers waiting to cash in on what's conservatively estimated as a four-billion-dollar (yes, billion) market. And this is, as they say, just the beginning.

SKIN

The biggest decision you have to make with regard to caring for your skin is not whether to do it (everybody, after all, washes his face), or even which of the going complexion philosophies to embrace, but simply how far to go with the whole business. Skin care—and by this we mean primarily the face though hands and neck are also deserving of your attention—can become a full-time occupation, making not only twice- or thrice-daily demands, but entailing in addition certainly biweekly, weekly, even monthly rituals. Do you have the time, money, and patience for all this?

The point is to do something good to your skin *regularly*. That something can be as simple as washing your face with a mild soap and warm water, once in the morning and again at night, or as complicated as a multi-phase regimen consisting of a soapy massage, alcohol splash, an acidiferous—yes, the skin is naturally acidic—bath, and an application of a moisturizer.

See how unreasonable things can begin to seem, given the exigencies of your own workaday life? It's not that anything we described just now is off-base but just that it runs the risk of becoming too much, of turning most busy, active men against the idea of proper skin care altogether, so that they return, disillusioned and a little self-righteous, to their old bar-of-Dial-soap-in-a-hot-shower solution. And that *is* off-base; in fact, downright deleterious.

Consequently, all we ask now is that you consider the following facts: the skin that covers your face is tender, made of protein, and full of tiny holes called pores. These three facts, taken together, make the facial skin a particularly easy mark for bacteria as well as for the machinations of your own endocrine system, and for your nervous and nutritional habits. So keep it clean. This means soap and water at least twice a day. More specifically, it means a mild soap, superfatted perhaps, if you have dry skin. This is the sort of thing a knowledgeable pharmacist can advise on. Work the soap into a lather in your hands and spread it onto and around your already moistened face. Rub thoroughly with your fingertips (no washcloths need apply), which will help to dissolve grease and loosen dead skin cells. Then rinse, more than once. Nothing dries out and dulls the skin more than a soapy residue.

Fine. The skin is clean and a little shiny. Now it's time to tone it, to make it look firm, smooth, and *poreless*. This is where the going gets a little rough: there are too many products, coupled with a welter of professional opinions and, for that matter, personal preferences on the part of friends. (Perhaps this is the right time to warn you against listening to anybody except professionals on the subject of what you should do to your face. This is a highly sensitive program you're devising, and your body chemistry and daily habits require a highly specific solution.) One thing you should at least consider, however, is the use of a gentle astringent. As soon as your face is dry, squeeze or pour some onto a cotton ball and draw the cotton ball over the entire surface of the face, concentrating especially on oily areas. This operation will minimize the size of your pores. An alternative is clarifying lotion, likewise alcohol-based but just a little stronger, which completes the removal of the dead cells of the skin's uppermost layer that washing with soap and water started.

Both kinds of products will refresh the skin, making it feel tingly and tighter, especially as the alcohol in them evaporates. But beware of labels on these and other cosmetic preparations, which have been notoriously loose in their use of what should be highly technical terms. "Astringent," for instance, implies but doesn't always guarantee the presence of aluminum salts. It's only now that such vaguenesses are beginning to be regulated by the Food and Drug Administration, and even when they are fully regulated you'll still need to understand what a particular label or, for that matter, a particular ingredient, signifies. There's a book on the market now that may help you called *The Consumer's Dictionary of Cosmetic Ingredients* by Ruth Winter, but if you're still unsure of a product's true nature or if you have known allergies to things chemical, check with your pharmacist. And eschew the advice of department-store salespeople who are likely to push their line of products no matter what.

Facial masks, which come in two basic forms, clay and gel, take toning one step further by stimulating circulation and leaving the skin with a healthy glow. The clay kind works much like a vacuum cleaner, picking up cellular debris that mere washing can't reach and absorbing leftover oil and dirt. Because of their overall strength, clay masks shouldn't be used more than once a week. Their gel counterparts, however, are gentle enough to be used daily, unless your skin is especially sensitive or you're trying to retain the pathetic vestiges of last summer's tan. One applies both masks in the same fashion, spreading the substance over the surface of the face carefully with the fingertips and always avoiding the delicate eye area. The clay mask is generally left on longer, perhaps as much as half an hour, then washed off. The gel one stays on only till dry, as little as ten minutes, and is then peeled off, like dead skin after a sunburn. The gel mask is particularly good for restoring moisture to dry skin, since it doesn't soak up oil and its taut filminess encourages the skin to store up water beneath it. Its effects, though, are more short-lived than the clay's; hence, the desirability of frequent use.

One more toning device to know about: the facial sauna, good for all skin types. To do it yourself, fill a large pot with water (we should mention that there's the option of adding herbs to this water, but we'll leave the matter of which herbs to you) and bring it to a boil. Now take the pot to a good steady table. Sit down in front of the pot, drape a towel over your head and shoulders, and lean over the steaming surface, your tented face roughly a foot above it. Remain thus for from five to ten minutes, coming up for air a couple of times during this period. The result? Skin that's plump, smooth, soft, and, for the moment, wrinkle-free.

The face-care trinity is completed by the lubricating you'll do to put back into the skin some of the desirable things that the cleaning and toning have, of necessity and with no malice, taken away from it. Now not every skin-care expert in the world believes in lubricating artificially what nature has provided with its own active oil and sweat glands, and it does seem clear that perfectly normal skin can become needlessly addicted to moisturizer and begin to behave in spoiled-child fashion. So if your skin is oil balanced or normal, which is to say it isn't red or flaky or simply dry to the touch, leave well enough alone. Apply a light, all-purpose lotion containing lanolin or similar animal oil, only when indoor heating or cold, windy weather has upset your facial equilibrium.

But if your skin is naturally dry, look for a thin, lotionlike cream that contains moisturizing agents to help the skin lock in water and wear it always, awake and asleep.

Don't worry too much about the change in seasons, though this is a voguish thing to do. A good lotion should work equally well winter and summer (though you may want to use extra on cold, dry days and ease up almost entirely in the humidity of August). And even very oily skin can use some help in the quick-to-dry-out areas around the eyes and mouth. Just be temperate and make sure to wipe off anything your skin doesn't seem to be ingesting. Why, after all, force-feed a goose that's already too fat?

There are a lot of men who, though more than willing to lavish time and money on their skin, don't feel like organizing their own regimens or who have skin that's genuinely troubled and looks as if it could stand some professional counsel. These men might consider what gives every indication of becoming a trend in men's grooming, whole lines of skin-care products sold in department stores and advertised in national publications. Aramis is certainly the most extensive, having in fact three separate lines geared to the degree of need. Clinique has just introduced a spin-off of its well-known women's line, a three-step system called Skin Supplies for Men, and Erno Laszlo is developing a male-oriented promotion of its highly individualized (and highly expensive) program. All of this will save you considerable uncertainty and even more shopping time.

And don't overlook the possibility of a professional facial for true deep-cleansing and reinvigoration. Three or four treatments a year, in combination with conscientious at-home care, will put an end to all but the most serious skin conditions. For these, and we can't stress this enough, you *must* visit a dermatologist. At the least, he'll help you devise a program of skin care, perhaps including prescription medication of a kind that would otherwise be unavailable to you. And while he's at it, he may uncover a problem that's systemic and simply choosing to reveal itself on that vulnerable face of yours.

Let's at this point assume that you've gotten your skin into a state of health whereby it can be worked with, made to conform ever so subtly to your ideas of who you are and how you should look. We're talking about design, of course, of making things look a little better than they would if left to their own devices. A little bit better, mind you; though plastic surgery and silicone injections may be valid as ways of dealing

ERNO LASZLO

The Erno Laszlo Institute was founded in the thirties by a Hungarian doctor. His system of skin care, probably the best around but very demanding and very expensive, requires that you become a member of the institute and acquire the preparations from one of the few specialty stores that sells them. The cornerstone of the system is the use of one of three special soaps and very, very hot water to cleanse the skin and open its pores, followed by an alcohol splash. The belief is that skin, when properly treated, can subsist nicely on its own powers of lubrication, without the haphazard use of moisturizers.

ARAMIS

Back in the mid-sixties Esteé Lauder, one of the biggest women's cosmetics houses, launched the Aramis division, which was designed to offer a far-reaching assortment of personal-care products for men. Shave foam, shampoo, conditioner, deodorant, cologne, and that important newcomer bronzer became available at major department stores— all endowed with the same spicy fragrance, as the women's line, all packaged in the same elegant, marbleized containers.

CLINIQUE

Like Aramis, Clinique is from the Esteé Lauder people. But of the two, only Clinique has a genuine dermatological slant. If your skin is troubled, Clinique is a perfect choice. Clinique Skin Supplies for Men—"clinically formulated" and "100-percent fragrance free," according to the label—provide their users with a system. Begin with Clinique soap, follow with the appropriate "scruffing" lotion to rid your face of excess oil and dead cellular debris, and finish with an application of moisturizer, enigmatically dubbed "M Lotion."

CASWELL-MASSEY

**Maybe you don't want to visit your local depart-
ment store's cosmetics section and spend from
$25 to $100 for a complete assortment of a single
manufacturer's products. In this case, go to the
best drugstore in town and assemble three or
four essential products for your skin. We headed
for Caswell-Massey, which bills itself as "the
oldest chemists and perfumers in America," and
with their help, wound up with the products you
see here. There are the makings for a gentle,
bracing almond-meal-and-witch-hazel mask, a
bar of Simple Soap (so-called because it contains
no perfume, coloring, or other additives), and
Creme Simon (from France) to lock in moisture.
The result: a complete daily program for normal-
to-dry skin.**

with ravaged or even merely inane facial
planes, they're not something you can
undertake in your own bathroom. You may
wonder what you can undertake.

Well, in truth, not much. It may be the
fourth quarter of a century notorious for
having enshrined both Rudolph Valentino
and Mick Jagger, but makeup for men is
still, with one exception, taboo in virtually
every social milieu. The exception is Bronzers, which have been with us for a decade,
more than enough time for them to have
become fixtures in many men's grooming
wardobes. And don't kid yourself: bronzers are makeup, nothing more nor less,
intended not to upgrade the health or vital-
ity of your skin but to transform the face itself
into something more nearly perfect than
what it wakes up being every morning.
How do they do this? By adding simple
color, of course, but more importantly by
playing up your face's contours.

This means that you don't slap the
bronzer just anywhere, nor do you necessarily apply it all over your face, as most
manufacturers recommend. Instead,
squeeze a little gel from the tube (solid or
stick bronzers are no longer sold) onto your
fingertips. Because almost all bronzers now
contain built-in moisturizers, smooth application shouldn't be a problem, but you
should be careful to blend the bronzer as
you apply it, first lightly over the surface of
the face, including the margins of brow and
cheeks, then down to the neck. Remember:
coloring doesn't stop abruptly at the jawline; blending from there on down is critical
if one isn't to be left with a telltale line of
demarcation.

When you're satisfied that the base coat
is even and subtle, it's time to think about
contouring. This means extra bronzer
along the cheekbones, down the bridge of
the nose, and across the brow, especially
just above the eyes, the very places that a
day in the sun would emphasize. Again,
blend carefully so the final effect is natural,
not theatrical.

Here are two additional face-making
tips, though you may not want to discuss

them in the office. Don't be afraid to trim eyebrows that are too bushy, using tweezers to root out hairs that have no business being where they are (over the nose, for instance, resulting in that one-long-eyebrow effect) and scissors to trim hairs that, though appropriately placed, are too long and profuse.

On days when black circles are a big problem, you can use a flesh-colored concealing stick (Erace is a popular one) to cover them over. Gently draw on under and around the eyes, from inner to outer corners, then blend with the fingertips. The stick is also handy for disguising blemishes when you're beyond Clearasil age.

That's it for now. Other male-oriented cosmetics are beginning to appear on the market and will, in time, probably gain some measure of acceptance. In the meantime, dash on some cologne (the one that's more or less your trademark), straighten those glasses (glasses frames are the only thing we can think of that are capable of doing as much for the structure of your face as a good beard), and get out the door. The party, the planning session, the flight to Paris—one of them's bound to be waiting.

HAIR

If we devote less space to hair care than to skin, it's not because it's less important but only that you've already given the matter some close attention. Within the last ten years or so, the American man has become extremely (some would say excessively) hair conscious. For one thing, the Beatles made hair into a very big business. Although the longer styles may have driven the corner barber out of business, they caused a whole new enterprise, the unisex hair salon, to flourish. Here, likely as not, one would have a glass of wine with one's haircut, and the haircut itself had expanded to include such heretofore female prerogatives as the shampoo, blow dry, and—even more scandalously—a permanent or color rinse. Of course, the Beatles didn't do it alone. In a way, they merely provided an example and gave concrete form to ideas of style that were probably already lurking in the backs of many young American minds, male or female.

Although most of the American man's attention has been focused on stylistic matters like cut and color, he's come to know that healthy hair and scalp are two cornerstones on which any truly fashionable appearance is based. And he knows that no amount of money invested in salon styling and fancy implementation is going to pay off unless he takes the time to treat his hair well. Here's a recap, then, of matters you're already essentially familiar with.

The basic goal with hair, as with skin, is to keep it clean. This means shampooing as often as necessary to prevent the accumulation of dulling oils and surface dirt in the hair and loose flakes on the scalp. In big cities shampooing can become a daily affair, especially for people with oily scalps (the result of overactive sebaceous glands). In such cases a mild shampoo—one based on castile soap, for instance—and a single lathering are preferred. But if your hair is relatively clean and your scalp normal or dry, you may shampoo as seldom as twice a week, in which case a stronger shampoo, as well as dual applications of it, is in order.

As for finding precisely the right shampoo, we're afraid you, like everyone else in the world, are on your own. Everyone, including the experts leading the pack, has different and often wildly contradictory ideas on the subject. Our only advice is to beware of shampoos that are militantly alkaline, since hair, like skin, has an acid mantle that must be respected. To test the alkalinity of a prospective shampoo (or any other liquid grooming aid), buy a packet of corn-colored Nitrazine testing papers at your pharmacy. Like pieces of litmus paper, these will indicate extreme alkalinity by turning blue when dipped into the liquid, a sure indication that the product is going to be too strong for all but the most resilient heads.

There are two things everybody should make a point of doing when shampooing: massage the scalp to bolster circulation and release tension, preferably before the shampoo, as hair is at its most vulnerable when wet and shouldn't then be subjected to the rigors of finger-and-wrist stimulation. And rinse thoroughly. Even when you're sure you've gotten all the suds out, rinse again. Any soapy residue is going to dull the hair's natural luster and may irritate the scalp, causing it to flake in a way that resembles mild dandruff.

You'll recall that with skin we asked you to worry about two separate processes: toning and lubricating. Hair requires both these actions as well but, mercifully, they can be done with a single substance, a conditioner. This is your prime ally in ensuring luster, manageability, and body (which will, by the way, make fine or thin hair seem more substantial). At the same time, it will counter any harsh or drying effects that the shampoo may have had, and it even helps camouflage split ends.

Herbal rinses leave your hair smelling fresh but you should be familiar with the herbs in question. Although it's unlikely they'll do any real harm, you may be paying through the nose for them. Protein conditioners make sense if your hair is thin, as they coat each shaft of hair, thereby increasing its girth and promoting a look of overall fullness. Body-building fluids, made of water and shellac, have a hair-spray-like effect. Though they're good disciplinarians, they can make the hair sticky and dull.

We're afraid you've got another shopping-around situation on your hands, but in this case you have a ready-made consultant: your haircutter. Whether he's a top-name stylist or a humble corner barber, he's familiar with hair and scalp problems and spends his life solving them, in fact. More than that: except for you, he's the only living expert on *your* hair and scalp. Don't think you're overstepping your bounds in asking him to recommend, even say a few words about, a shampoo and conditioner to meet your special needs. Of course, in the case of special scalp problems that go beyond the formation of controllable flakes, consultation with a full-fledged dermatologist is de rigueur.

That said, let's pass to the aspect of hair that has all of us at least partially in its thrall, that (from our vantage point, anyway) never fails to fascinate, to elicit responses from friends and strangers alike. We're referring, of course, to the fact that hair is the most alterable and hence most *designable* part of your body. It can convey to the rest of the world the message you want to put over. Or it can betray you utterly.

Your options today are almost infinite. You can let your hair grow to your shoulders or prune it to within a fraction of an inch of your skull. You can wear it full and lush, making it your most visible feature, or slick it back so that your eyes and bone structure are thrown into dramatic relief. You can highlight it, even superimpose an alien hue on it, for a night of fantasy or a quarter-year of commitment. Where do you begin? With the best hairstylist you can find.

You've been told this before, and it's true. There's just no substitute for the person in your life who understands what you want to look like, what you're capable of looking like, and how to get from the one to the other. Technique is essential but useless, unless he can grasp the nature of what you want from him. Here are some guidelines, then, for finding this stylist:

□ Talk to men whose hair you'd like to have for your own. Find out who did it and where that person can be found.

□ At the same time, familiarize yourself with the salons in your town and know what each one's specialty is—easy naturalness, stylized rarefaction, geometric precision, and so on.

□ Plan to have a conversation with the stylist once you've met him. You can expect

EIGHT IMAGINATIVE SOLUTIONS TO PROBLEM HAIR

Problem: Straight hair that hangs limp and becomes flat in summer heat.

Solution: A mild, acid-balanced, curly permanent restructures the hair for an easy style that needs only shampooing, towel drying, and finger shaping to stay neat.

Process: The hair is wrapped on perm rods to control size of curls, but in a nonpattern to avoid an artificial look. After processing and neutralizing, a rinse of tomato juice returns hair's normal acidity. Next is a cut to blend the curl.

Problem: Red highlights which look unnatural when bleached by the sun. He also has an uneven hairline and cowlicks.

Solution: Color toning with a semipermanent rinse disguises the red. A center part controls the hair. Cream conditioners kept on the hair during sun exposure help retard fading. At night, styling gels keep the look sleek.

Process: Shampoo-in color, custom-blended. A blunt, balanced cut.

Problem: Wispy, fine hair that often looks lifeless during hectic activity in the sun.

Solution: Body waving adds the necessary extra lift and control by retexturing the hair while adding bulk and movement.
Process: A very mild perm to give body but not curl. A geometric style to frame the face.

Problem: Thick, tightly curled hair that requires blow-drying after every shampoo to give fullness and shape. When damp the hair shrinks and must be blown and picked again, risking damage from excessive heat.

Solution: Afro perming with a mild relaxer is less time-consuming and less likely to burn the hair than harsh chemical straighteners. Curl is redirected from tight to loose. No blow-drying required.
Process: Cream is applied to the hair with a shampoo brush and the hair is relaxed to the desired curl. Then the hair is neutralized with a nonalkaline shampoo and conditioned. Finally, it's cut and shaped.

Problem: Fine, dense hair that requires a lot of blow-drying, since it tends to be unmanageable and lose its shape. Excessive blow-drying was taking moisture from the hair, leaving it brittle.

Problem: Naturally wavy hair that's a drab, lusterless brown. Summer humidity makes the hair less manageable.

Solution: Body perming his long hair gives it shape and provides control so upkeep is minimal. Shampoo, towel dry, and arrange hair casually with the fingers.
Process: The hair is rolled on large rods, then saturated with a mild, acid-balanced perming lotion. Heat activates the curl. After neutralizing, the hair is organically conditioned.

Solution: Color weaving enhances the brown by brightening more than lightening. Conditioner makes maintenance easy.
Process: Hair is examined for natural light accents. These will be lightened more. Then individual hair strands are "woven" by a comb to select the random shafts to be treated by two to three different lightening shades. On brown hair the tints are in the bronze/gold family. Paintbrush application further controls the subtle changes. As only a small percentage of hair is permanently tinted, the regrowth pattern isn't jarring. The hair is treated with a conditioning shampoo, then styled. A short, carefree style to be towel dried and shaped with the fingers is achieved by selective layered cutting.

Problem: Weakly pigmented hair easily faded by the sun's intense ultraviolet rays. The sandy-blond color lightens so rapidly that it appears stripped by peroxide. The length, combined with the effect of solar rays, makes the hair dry and brittle.

Solution: Color treating the hair with bronze henna (standard henna adds more red) initially darkens the hair slightly, while protecting it against extensive sun-fading. Thus the hair sun-washes with a more natural appearance as summer progresses.

Process: Mixed with water, henna makes a paste which is applied to the hair. A vegetable-based permanent, stain, and natural conditioner, henna works by heat from a sun lamp. The hair is then cut in layers for body.

Problem: Fine, oily hair requiring constant shampooing and blow-drying to keep it from clinging to his head and looking flat.

Solution: Color styling is not only a head start on sun-tipping, but the easy lightening in combination with the cut actually lifts the hair from the scalp.

Process: Colorist and cutter plan where the mild bleach is to be applied with a paintbrush to accent the layer cut.

him to be cunning but not clairvoyant. Let him know what you have in mind, even if you're not sure that your hair will cooperate or that you can carry it off. This is where his expertise is invaluable.

☐ Insist on meeting him while you're wearing your old hair and your street clothes so that he can get an overall idea of what you look like and how you're in the habit of putting yourself together.

☐ Before the actual cutting begins, the two of you should come to an agreement as to what the outcome of the cut will be. This means that he should give some evidence of understanding what you're saying when you talk about your hair. Or, alternatively (and equally validly), you should be willing to put yourself in his hands completely, deferring to his judgment and experience.

☐ Watch him as he cuts. He should be, above all else, precise in his movements. If what he does mystifies you or seems to be in blatant opposition to what you've agreed upon, stop him and state your reservations.

☐ Don't expect a lot of socializing while you're there in the chair. He's there to cut your hair, not entertain you. It's not even his job to put you at ease, beyond displaying competence and self-confidence, of course.

☐ One last thing: If what your cutter has done looks complicated or is simply unfamiliar to you, ask him how you can maintain the style at home, what brushes, conditioners, and the like you should have in stock and what techniques with regard to drying you should master.

As to what kind of cut to get—well, you know as well as we do how confused the marketplace is these days. In general, long (i.e., shoulder-length) hair seems a bit passé, requiring a lot of bravado to carry off. Short hair, from the eighth-of-an-inch "convict cut" to a relatively luxuriant two-inch-with-side-part model, makes a great deal of sense, combining functionalism and ease of maintenance with an aura of masculine modesty. The cut can even be made to seem elegant if a little length is left along the nape of the neck. However, short hair

does little for the person with a defect or two to conceal. If your face is too long or too broad, your nose or ears a little on the big side, your head not well shaped, then consider medium-length hair shaped in a way that camouflages rather than exacerbates the problem. A certain fullness, especially if the hair is shiny and precisely cut, can compensate for any number of evils.

Now on to a couple of truly thorny topics: curl and color. First, keep in mind that unless these are very subtly done, they're going to be considered extreme and possibly ridiculous measures by people who already know you. If that's your intention, fine; we all have the right to alter our appearance, even drastically, if we want to. But if you want at the same time to hang on to your legitimacy within an existing social order, then easy—and gradually—does it is the best possible advice.

We'd like to be able to tell you that hair coloring and the permanent/straightening business are as painless and risk-free as a good shampooing, but they're not. Unless a close friend is a trained beautician, you owe it to yourself and to your family and friends to seek paid professional attention. The chemical processes involved tend to be complex and irreversible (the hair's molecular composition is, in fact, being tampered with), and it's well worth the extra money to have an expert in attendance. Exceptions to this include color rinses and semipermanent tinting agents, which are both mild and temporary and which you really can handle yourself. But read the package carefully. Remember that the instructions printed on it are there not to amuse but to protect you from your own worst instincts.

And in the event of confusion, specialized needs, or natural reticence, consult that person who knows all about hair in general and yours in particular, the one you went to such lengths to find: your stylist. He should be as knowledgeable about color and curl as he is about cut. He may even have a colleague who's a specialist.

SHAVING

The only difference between a man's skin and a woman's is that the former can, in certain places, sprout whiskers. Nor is the skin underneath those whiskers any less sensitive or tender than that of the cheeks or brow. This means that shaving, perhaps a man's most basic grooming act (at least in the comparatively hairless twentieth century), can't afford to be unconsidered. Whether done with an electric razor or with lather and blade, the secret lies in making the proper preparations.

In the case of the electric method, it's tempting to shave before washing the face, thereby assuring yourself of a dry surface. But don't be lazy. Beards that haven't been preconditioned are not going to come off as cleanly as those that have. So wash your face and neck first, then rinse well and dry as thoroughly as possible. Now use an electric preshave lotion over the same area to remove stubborn residual moisture. The preshave also reduces friction between the skin and the shaving head, reducing the likelihood of nicks and abrasions, and it stiffens beard hairs so that they can be cut off right at the skin line.

A wet shave is more sensual and, in a sense, easier. It's at its absolute best after a long, hot shower. Apply shaving cream, available in both the familiar aerosol can and the more old-fashioned tube, liberally to all relevant areas. Let it stand for a couple of minutes while the cream lubricates the skin and softens the beard. Wet your razor with water as hot as you can stand and, not pressing too hard, shave in the direction of your beard growth. Keep in mind, however, that your beard changes its direction as it travels over your face and that sometimes beard hairs can grow in opposite directions, even from follicle to follicle. So gentleness is in order. When you're done, rinse your face first with warm, then with cold water. This will help close the pores. Splash on a little after-shave to soothe, heal, and restore the skin's acid balance and you're ready to go.

BEARDS AND MUSTACHES

Of course this is the perfect time to remind you of perhaps your most important design option in the entire personal-appearance showroom—facial hair. What's entailed is the cessation or at least relaxation of the shaving techniques just discussed. As you've no doubt realized, beards and mustaches (and, to a lesser degree, sideburns) have, as ways of customizing your face, no real competition. They correct any number of facial faults—weak chin, unexceptional cheekbones, incipient jowls—and emphasize two of everybody's potentially most marketable features: the eyes and mouth. Also, they provide an amusing deviation from one's prior appearance history, a deviation that can, initially, border on out-and-out disguise.

Some cautions are nevertheless in order. Taller man can carry off a greater volume of hair on both face and head than short ones. If you're small, cut your beard and mustache close to the face. If you're particularly weak featured, consider trimming your beard and mustache in a way that's sharp and crisp. If your features are already overwhelming, whether too dramatic or simply too big, opt for a gentler, less consciously designed effect.

And don't lose sight of the person you are and the things you do. If you spend most of your time in a business suit, a wild and woolly beard will make you look like a lumberjack on his way to church. Visual contrast is fine if you live a life that rewards it. Otherwise, better stick to the cultivation of a

CHOOSING THE RIGHT BEARD OR MUSTACHE TO FIT YOUR FACE

IRREGULAR NOSE, JAGGED CHEEKBONES
A full beard evens out irregularities by providing facial balance. It also gives the nose character while diminishing its prominence. Irregularities and "defects" are transformed into points of interest.

PROTRUDING JAW, FULL LOWER LIP
Utilize the strength of the chin here and add power to the upper lip via a full mustache with tips angled upward.

TRIANGULAR CHIN, TIGHT LIPS
A full beard can soften severe features and square off a pointy chin. Some men even perm straight hair for an overall rounded frame.

HIGH NOSE, NEUTRAL CHEEKBONES
A mustache adds width and definition to the face by contouring hollows. The most effective mustache here is one that's strong and full. A slight upward tilt at the ends helps too.

PUG NOSE, BROAD CHEEKBONES
With a small nose the mustache should be flat. Too much fullness and the nose will get lost. Clipping is crucial. It's not necessary to fill the entire space between nose and top lip. Keep the mustache small and neat.

LONG NOSE, SOFT CHEEKBONES
If the face is overpowered by the hairstyle, redirect the focus via a beard or mustache. But make it a trimmed beard or mustache. Heavy facial hair can overwhelm the face. Careful shaping and shaving add character.

SQUARE JAW, SENSUAL LIPS
When the face is broad, a downward-tilted mustache alters the lines. The sensuality of the lips remains but the new effect becomes decidedly stronger.

FLABBY CHIN, MINOR MOUTH
A mustache disguises the mouth, while a beard creates a jawline—both leading to a stronger image. If your eyes are good, they'll show up to better advantage without the distraction of a weak chin. Avoid shaved-in straight lines, except on the neck. Shorter hair also prevents a top-heavy look.

NARROW FOREHEAD, LOW HAIRLINE
A low hairline looks best with minimal facial hair. A beard is too strong, but a well-groomed mustache can direct attention away from the forehead and balance the weight of the face.

WIDE FOREHEAD, RECEDING HAIRLINE
A carefully groomed beard and mustache can make the hairline look good—certainly better than tricks to camouflage it. A frame is achieved that focuses attention on the face instead of on the thinning hair.

FLAT FOREHEAD, IRREGULAR HAIRLINE
Attention is shifted from the forehead by a full beard or even a mustache. Facial hair adds vigor, making the hairline interesting rather than a grooming problem.

BALD
If a man is bald, he should definitely eliminate the resulting facial blandness by growing a countenance-strengthening mustache.

single consonant image. Here, as everywhere in the arena of personal style, appropriateness counts.

Once you've made the decision to grow a beard or mustache, be prepared for a few weeks of uncertainty. Beards grow in at rates that vary greatly, from person to person and from facial section to facial section. Patchiness, which often seems irreversible at first, ceases to be a problem as whiskers grow longer and able to cover over neighboring hairless areas. Most important, with length and fullness comes the opportunity to shape the beard so that it sets off your facial structure. When you do shape it, be cognizant of where your facial curves and angles lie. Conceal them if you like, but don't make them compete with the lines of the beard. Facial hair should consolidate the bottom half of your face, not further segment it.

Two practical hints for risk-free shaping. Never attempt to cut a wet beard or mustache, as water-logged whiskers never lie the same way they would when dry. And don't be hasty with that razor and scissors. Rather, work slowly, gradually, by trial and error, perhaps even using an eyebrow pencil to sketch in the lines you think you'll want to cut along. Remember that with a single rash move you can undo three months' waiting.

Remember, too, that the skin under a beard differs from that covering the rest of the face only in being hidden. It's tender, it's susceptible to nervous and bacterial eruptions, and it has to be kept clean. Use a gentle shampoo and feel free to wash your beard with it every time you take a shower. Brushing the beard is in order, too. Use a firm-bristled brush and equally firm downward strokes, being careful not to irritate the skin below.

One final word. Have your beard trimmed every time you get a haircut—even just a trim—so that the proportions of your head, and especially your silhouette, remain constant. And if you get a radically different haircut, you'll probably want to rethink completely the whole business of having a beard and/or mustache, perhaps even shaving it off. The face, after all, is a unity, not a grab bag of competing features.

APPENDIX 1

ALL YOU NEED TO KNOW ABOUT THE PERFECT FIT

One of the more encouraging truisms of fashion is that proper fit can turn the most budget-conscious clothes purchases into garments with a look and feel akin to custom work. While you obviously won't get functional buttonholes on a jacket sleeve or a shirt collar that fits exactly, your clothes and accessories can be tailored specifically to fit you.

To turn yourself out as a properly fitted individual you must start at the beginning—with shirt and shoes. These items are determining factors in the proper fitting of a suit, sport coat, or trousers, and they must fit properly before you proceed to the more involved garments.

So, here are our exclusive guidelines for a perfect, elegant fit.

SUITS AND SPORT COATS

There's more to the proper fitting of a suit or sport coat than the likes of sleeve length and inseam measurements. A lot depends on where or how you intend wearing the garment. Consider these points:

☐ Will you wear the garment for business, travel, leisure, et cetera?
☐ Will you wear the garment indoors with a regular shirt; outdoors with a heavy shirt or sweater; both?
☐ Do you want a precise, formal appearance or a more relaxed image?
☐ Are there special items you'll want to carry with you when you wear the garment? If so, take them with you when you go for the fitting.
☐ What shoes will you wear with the garment—regular heel height; thick, heavy soles; higher heels? These differences will affect the length of trousers.
☐ What type of shirt will you be wearing? How the jacket lapels lay along the shirt collar affects how the jacket looks. And with proper sleeve length you'll be able to see exactly how much cuff will show.
☐ And your underwear—will you wear boxer style, or briefs? The fit is different.

THE TRY-ON

Let a salesman guide you to the correct size, but since you're the only person who's going to wear the garment, you must decide whether the fit feels correct for your body. Some salesmen have been known to "clean up" a garment via some judicious and usually undetected smoothing and adjusting of certain key areas that may lead the unwary to believe a garment fits when actually it only appears so. This maneuver may also include the salesman positioning himself between you and the mirror when you put on the jacket. Make sure you have an unobstructed three-way view of yourself in the mirror and adjust the jacket yourself.

The first points of fit to check in a jacket are the way the collar lies in back and the lay of the lapels in front. Slip on the jacket and fasten the middle button, making certain the collar lies close to your shirt collar around the back of the neck. To accomplish this, bring your arms forward and up over your head. This will force the collar of the jacket against the shirt collar; if the collar contact remains the same when you lower your arms, the jacket has passed the first test of fit.

In front the lapels should ride without buckling, close to your shirt collar, the lapels anchoring the edge of the collar at

The fit of a vest should be smooth and close to the body without the least sign of pulling or creasing. The last button is always left undone. You may, if you wish, add a slim, gold watch chain for an extra touch of elegance.

Lapels should lie smoothly, without buckling or bulging. Bear in mind that while lapels are currently narrowing, a medium width is always a good investment. Collar pins make a shirt look crisp, whether you opt for the eyelet variety pictured or the fasten-on type.

Flashing a discreet length of shirt cuff is one of those debatable fashion questions. Today, half an inch—or shall we say 1.27 centimeters?—is appropriate. Of course, it's all really a matter of correct proportions, of balancing the length with the rest of your attire.

Another nicety to consider is the break of your trousers, particularly relevant if they're without cuffs. Provided you're neither short nor heavy (in which case it will tend to emphasize the shape you're in) a break is logical. How it breaks depends upon the fabric. You should also remember that if you fit a pair of trousers while wearing dress shoes, the break will occur at a different point or not at all from when you're wearing, say, short boots.

The cuff, having come on strong in recent years, may be taken as a classic touch for the foreseeable future. Although fluctuations are certainly acceptable, something between 1¾ and 2 inches is the preferred margin. Generally, patterned trousers look best with a narrower cuff, whereas fine wools in winter or linens and cottons in summer benefit from a greater width. Trousers that are cuffed can also have a slight break, but this again is optional.

1

2

3

When trying on a new jacket, raise your arms above your head (1), then bring them slowly down to your sides (2, 3). This settles the jacket on the shoulders, enabling you to judge by the way the coat hangs whether you'll experience a fit problem. These movements also reveal collar problems, discernible if the fabric bunches in that area.

the collar bone. When you move your shoulders up, down, and around, the jacket should be in close contact but not binding—across the shoulders, around the shoulders, and under the arms. If these areas feel and look right, proceed with the fitting; if not, try another size or style.

When you've decided on the appropriate size and model, put the suit on and place all necessary items in the pockets of the jacket and trousers. Now you're ready to meet the fitter.

Your fitter can make or break the look of your garment, so relate to him. Give him an idea of the activities you'll be involved in while wearing the garment; any special physical or aesthetic requirements; the degree of closeness you prefer in the fit. Acknowledge his skill and work with him. Agree mutually to the extent and areas of alteration and be sure that what he writes on the alteration ticket is what you have agreed upon. (Note: a single chalk mark indicates a reduction in length or size; a single mark with double crosshatches means an expansion. The letters R.C. written anywhere on the alteration ticket simply mean Remove Chalk, so beware.) To make certain the finished garment will meet your expectations, ask the fitter to pin the areas being altered as he proceeds with the fitting.

ALTERATIONS

Jacket. When the appropriate alterations have been pinned, the jacket should ride smoothly across the shoulders in front and back with no vertical, horizontal, or diagonal wrinkles or creases. (A good rule to follow in fitting trousers as well as jackets is that horizontal creases usually mean the garment is too tight; vertical creases indicate the garment is too loose, and in jackets, diagonal creases in the shoulder area generally mean that you, like most people, have one low shoulder, and the jacket should be altered accordingly, usually by padding.)

The collar and lapels should lie close to and smoothly on the back and sides of your shirt collar (one-half to three-quarters of an inch of collar showing in the back); and the jacket—to the point of flare—should be close to the body all around without any stress. Sleeves should be trim (no horizontal dimples or pulling on the upper arm where the sleeves meet the body of the jacket) and of the proper length. The length is measured from the tip of your thumb to the tip of the jacket sleeve—usually about five inches—leaving one-half to three-quarters of an inch of shirt cuff showing. (Since you have already altered your shirt sleeves to the correct length, the jacket sleeve will be the proper length to expose enough of the shirt cuff.) Aside from the fact that the visible shirt cuff makes a positive fashion statement, it protects the jacket cuff from undue wear and soil, thus minimizing the necessity for overly frequent cleaning. (On an overcoat, the sleeves should be long enough to cover the shirt cuff.)

Just as silhouette and details differ in suit jackets, so does length. The rule about the jacket meeting a point on your hand is an unreliable measure of proportion; since jacket lengths vary considerably, rely on your eye and the fitter's advice. Generally, the jacket should just cover your seat, although some hacking-type models will be longer and some of the newest designs markedly shorter. Longer jackets tend to shorten the silhouette, shorter lengths to give a leggier look. By selecting the proper long, regular, or short model you shouldn't require much, if any, alteration of the jacket length. (In most stores this alteration, if needed, is charged to the customer; most others are free.)

Trousers. The drop—or difference between the jacket size and the trouser waist measurement—can vary between four and eight inches on any given suit. If your waist measurement is one clothing manufacturers consider average for the size of your shoulders and chest, you'll probably need only minor waist and seat alterations.

The back of the jacket is another telltale area when it comes to judging fit. Vertical wrinkles (1) indicate that the jacket is too loose. Horizontal wrinkles (2) show it to be too tight. The same rules apply to trousers (3).

1

2

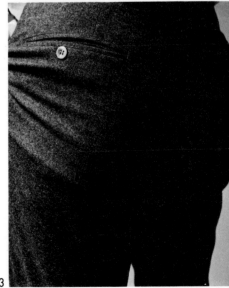

3

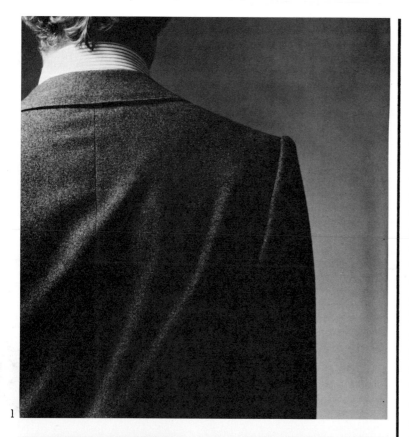

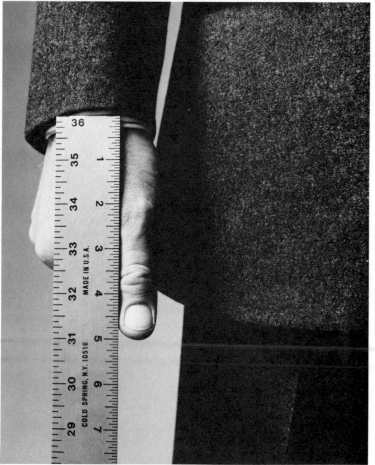

However, the greater the difference between the two measurements, the greater your problem, sometimes necessitating what's called a trouser recut. (This alteration is usually charged to the customer.)

There's a balance between the amount of fabric that should be taken in on the sides of the trousers and in the seat. The maximum reduction for the inseam (down the inside of the legs) is about one to one and one-half inches and two inches in the seat. If the trousers are still too full across the hips, the fitter can take in the outseam (down the outside of the legs). Watch the spacing of the trouser pockets. A recut is necessary if the hip pockets fall too close to the back center seam or if the side pockets fall too far back, making them uncomfortable to reach into. And remember, the tighter the fit through the waist, seat, and hips, the worse the wrinkling of the crotch area as you wear the suit. This, of course, necessitates frequent pressing which, taking into consideration the strain on fabric and seams, can shorten the life of the trousers.

Width. Custom trousers measure about nineteen inches at the knee and about twenty inches at the bottom. These widths vary somewhat from suit to suit.

Bottoms. For plain-bottom trousers it's recommended that the front rest and break slightly on the instep of your shoe, then slant three-quarters of an inch to one inch down to the back. If you prefer cuffs, two and one-quarter to two and one-half inches is considered a correct width. Cuffs on odd trousers that have exceptionally wide legs often run to a depth of three inches.

Diagonal lines along the back of the jacket (1) indicate that the opposite shoulder is too low. Correct sleeve length (2) measures 5 inches from end of sleeve to tip of thumb.

SHIRTS

The fit of ready-made shirts has come a long way since the time excess fabric was neatly hidden away by means of the military fold—executed by gathering the extra fabric at the waist into two equal folds along the side seams and smoothly folding the front around the sides and against the back of the body. This method worked well as long as a jacket was worn; otherwise it presented an untidy V-shaped overlay of fabric in the back. For the more affluent and fastidious, this folding gave way to tapering—first the simple practice of taking in the sides; and eventually the darting of the back (borrowed from the Italians to produce a super fit).

Today manufacturers build in a degree of taper that generally produces a curve starting at the chest, narrowing approximately five to six inches at the waist, and widening again to match the width of the shirt bottom to the chest dimension:

	Chest	Waist
Small	37"	31–32"
Medium	42"	36–37"
Large	46"	41–42"
	Tail	Collar
Small	37"	14½"
Medium	42"	15½"
Large	46"	16½"

The manufacturer's use of pleats or darts in a ready-made shirt doesn't change these measurements. Although they come as close as possible to fitting the wide range of body dimensions manufacturers must accommodate, it produces less than satisfactory fit for those whose measurements fall outside the averages. Only a custom shirtmaker can adequately produce a perfectly fitting shirt—proper size, style, and set of collar, body shape and sleeve length—but some simple alterations can produce the next best thing. If you're the self-sufficient type, and have access to a sewing machine, you can probably do the job yourself; otherwise have it done by an expert.

ALTERATIONS

Body. The simplest alteration is performed on the side seams. Turn the shirt inside out and pin the seams equally on both sides from under the arm to the bottom of the tail. Open the seams and sew along the pinned lines, reconstructing the original double-fold seam. This seam is more difficult than joining the two pieces face-to-face and stitching a simple seam, but it produces a much sturdier fastening and a more finished appearance.

The addition of two darts in the back can further smooth its fit from the small of the back up over the shoulder blades. The line of the dart is deepest at the waistline and should narrow smoothly in both directions from that point until it disappears at either end. Each dart should be spaced equally from the two side seams following the line and contour of the heavy back muscles. *Caution:* Fit can be too tight—the true elegance of fit is in smoothness in all positions. A specially tapered shirt can appear beautifully smooth and form-fitting while you're standing erect, but if it's too tight it will pull at the buttons and bind you into a potato-sack look when you're seated. To avoid this pitfall allow a four-inch excess of fabric over skin at the exhaling state.

Sleeves. The most precise way to shorten a sleeve (and the only really satisfactory method) is by taking the sleeve off the body of the shirt and cutting away the necessary amount from the top of the sleeve, then reattaching. The sleeve length is correct if the cuff falls lightly against the top of the hand between the bones that connect hand to wrist (arms hanging down at your sides). The problem of cuffs riding up when your arms are in motion can be overcome by fitting the cuff to your wrist and making the sleeve a half to one inch too long. The fitted cuff prevents the sleeve from extending over your hand, and the excess fabric accommodates your arm's movement.

When tapering a shirt, turn it inside out and pin along the side seams (1). This enables you to judge precisely how much fabric has to be trimmed. The properly fitted collar (2) hugs the neck without bulging, buckling, or wrinkling. A well-fitted shoulder should lie smoothly without stretching between shoulder blades (3). There should be no wrinkles in the sleeve.

1

2

3

SHOES

Since altering the fit of shoes is impossible—pads and fillers are stopgap measures at best and are never really satisfactory—you have only one chance to get it right. And since it's now impossible to check the fit visually through the magic of X ray (the exciting machine that enabled us to see every bone in the foot left more than a few shoe salesmen with skin cancer of the hand), it becomes a matter of feel—is there enough room in front to wiggle your toes; does the heel fit well into the back of the shoe; does the instep get firm support all around?

Today's shoe fashions often have little to do with proper fit and balance; but if you're willing to sacrifice some of the former for more of the latter, here are the things to keep in mind.

Balance. The weight of the body is divided on each foot at 50 percent on the heel, 30 percent on the big toe area or ball of the foot, and 20 percent on the little toe area. Therefore, a wide toe box with sufficient height is important for proper weight balance. A narrow toe area squeezes the toes together, diminishing your balance.

Heel. A heel taller than one and one-half inches is too high. It shifts the weight of the body too directly onto the toe area, driving the toes into the front of the shoe.

The longer the heel from front to back the better the balance. The heel should support the foot solidly from the back of the foot to the point directly under the ankle bone. The inside edge of the shoe heel should approximate a straight line, beyond the arch indentation to the point at which the big toe joins the foot.

Position. The proper positioning of the foot within the shoe (the foundation of the fit) depends upon the area around the instep. If this area fits properly it will feel snug and close to the foot all the way around. It's this fit that holds the ball of the foot at the widest part of the shoe, keeps the heel well into the back of the shoe, and the toes from sliding into the end of the shoe.

APPENDIX 2

THE GQ SHOPPER

Now that you've seen the best, here's where you can buy it. These are the stores across the country that stock the kind of merchandise you've seen in the pages of *Manstyle*, and which are featured regularly in *Gentlemen's Quarterly*. Are you ready? Then let's take it from the top—geographically speaking, that is.

THE NORTHEAST

NEW YORK CITY

ABRAHAM & STRAUS
420 Fulton Street, Brooklyn
BLOOMINGDALE'S
1000 Third Avenue, Manhattan
BARNEY'S
7th Avenue at 17th Street, Manhattan
CAMOUFLAGE
141 Eighth Avenue, Manhattan
CHARIVARI
2345 Broadway, Manhattan
PAUL STUART
Madison Avenue at 45th Street, Manhattan
SAKS FIFTH AVENUE
5th Avenue at 49th Street, Manhattan
SAN FRANCISCO
975 Lexington Avenue, Manhattan
STEVE'S
172 Spring Street, Manhattan
STONE FREE
754 Madison Avenue, Manhattan
105 W. 72nd Street, Manhattan
UNIQUE CLOTHING WAREHOUSE
716–720 Broadway, Manhattan
RIDING HIGH
1170 First Avenue, Manhattan

MASSACHUSETTS

BOSTON
FILENE'S
426 Washington Street
JORDAN MARSH
450 Washington Street

MARTINI & CARL
310 Boylston Street

CAMBRIDGE
THE CAMEL'S HUMP
18 Brattle Street

CHESTNUT HILL
LOUIS
Chestnut Hill

WORCESTER
TANNED HANDS
143 Highland Street

PENNSYLVANIA

PHILADELPHIA
AL BERMAN
54th & City Line Avenue (one of several Berman stores in Philadelphia)
DIMENSIONS
1627 Chestnut Street
JOHN WANAMAKER
1300 Market Street
STRAWBRIDGE & CLOTHIER
8th & Market Streets

PITTSBURGH
BROOKS BROTHERS
600 Smithfield Street
JOSEPH HORNE
Penn Avenue & Stanwix Street
ROBERT SWAN
5520 Walnut Street

CONNECTICUT

WESTPORT
COMMON MARKET
Village Square

WEST HARTFORD
J AND R POLLACK
28 LaSalle Road

WASHINGTON, D.C., AND ENVIRONS

BRITCHES OF GEORGETOWN
1247 Wisconsin Avenue N.W.
GARFINKEL'S
1401 F Street N.W.
WOODWARD AND LOTHROP
10th, 11th, F & G Streets N.W.

SPRINGFIELD, VA.
BRITCHES OF GEORGETOWN
Springfield Mall

McLEAN, VA.
BRITCHES OF GEORGETOWN
Tyson's Corner Center

VIRGINIA BEACH, VA.
ALEXANDER-BEEGLE
207 Laskin Road

BETHESDA, MD.
BRITCHES OF GEORGETOWN
Montgomery Mall, 7101 Democracy Boulevard

THE SOUTH

NORTH CAROLINA

ASHEVILLE
HUNTER & COGGINS
Merrimon Avenue
HUNTER & COGGINS
Hendersonville Road

CHARLOTTE
JODHPURS
Eastland Mall

CHAPEL HILL
JULIAN'S COLLEGE SHOP
140 E. Franklin Street

SOUTH CAROLINA

COLUMBIA
BRITTON'S
1337 Main Street
BRITTON'S
Dutch Square
BRITTON'S
Richland Mall
LYTLE PRESSLEY
1201 Main Street

GEORGIA

ATLANTA
BRITCHES OF GEORGETOWN
Lenox Square, 3393 Peachtree Road N.E.
J. RIGGINGS
2683 Peachtree Square
MUSES (George Muse Clothing Co.)
52 Peachtree Street
RICH'S, INC.
Broad & Alabama Streets

FLORIDA

MIAMI
BURDINE'S
22 E. Flagler Street
JORDAN MARSH
1501 Biscayne
THE 24 COLLECTIONS
Northeast 2nd Avenue, corner 24th Street

TAMPA
MAAS BROTHERS
Franklin & Zack Streets

KENTUCKY

LOUISVILLE
LEVY BROS.
235 W. Market Street

TENNESSEE

KNOXVILLE
M. S. McCLELLAN
1838 W. Cumberland
M. S. McCLELLAN
West Town Mall

LOUISIANA

NEW ORLEANS
MAISON BLANCHE
901 Canal Street
RUBENSTEIN BROS.
102 St. Charles Avenue

THE SOUTHWEST

TEXAS

AUSTIN
MAYA
1616 Lavaca

DALLAS
NEIMAN-MARCUS
Main & Ervay Streets
SANGER-HARRIS
303 N. Akard at Pacific
OUTFITTERS
428 North Park Center

HOUSTON
FOLEY'S
1110 Main Street
JOSKE'S
4925 Westheimer

LESLIE AND CO.
1749 S. Post Oak Road
SAKOWITZ
1111 Main Street
TOOTSIE'S
5350 Westheimer

ARIZONA

PHOENIX
DIAMOND'S
4501 E. Thomas Avenue

TUCSON
THE IRON TREE
1927 E. Speedway

NEW MEXICO

ALBUQUERQUE
ALAN'S APPAREL
57 Encantada Square N.E.
THOMAS JULIAN LTD.
3100 Juan Tabo N.E.

OKLAHOMA

OKLAHOMA CITY
CYRK
50 Penn Place

TULSA
B. HALL & LONG
510 S. Boston

THE MIDWEST

MICHIGAN

DETROIT
J. L. HUDSON CO.
1206 Woodward Avenue
SCHOLNICK'S
1400 Washington Boulevard

ROYAL OAK
ME AND MY LADY
1234 S. Woodward

WISCONSIN

MILWAUKEE
MAC NEIL & MOORE
770 N. Jefferson

MAC NEIL & MOORE
113 E. Silversprings Drive

WAUWATOSA (MILWAUKEE COUNTY)
MAC NEIL & MOORE
Mayfair Mall, 2500 N. Mayfair Road

MINNESOTA

MINNEAPOLIS
DAYTON'S
700 Nicollet Mall

IOWA

DES MOINES
BADOWER'S
2817 Ingersoll

ILLINOIS

CHICAGO
BASKIN CLOTHING CO.
137 S. State Street
BRITTANY LTD.
642 N. Michigan
HART, SCHAFFNER AND MARX
36 S. Franklin Street
I. MAGNIN
830 N. Michigan Avenue
MARSHALL FIELD
111 N. State Street
MORRY'S Menswear Inc.
645 N. Michigan
ULTIMO
114 East Oak Street

DECATUR
BACHRACH'S
2220 E. Wood Street

JOLIET
AL BASKIN CO.
201 N. Ottawa Street

WILMETTE
LONDON CORNER
1515 Sheridan Road

INDIANA

INDIANAPOLIS
THE GENTRY'S FOOTMAN
1742 E. 86th Street
D. DANN'S
111 N. Pennsylvania
1325 W. 86th Street

OHIO

CINCINNATI
DINO'S
16 E. Sixth
SHILLITO'S
7th & Race Streets

CLEVELAND
HIGBEE'S
100 Public Square
KNICKERBOCKER'S
2101 Richmond Road

COLUMBUS
GORDON ST. JOHN
6170 Busch Boulevard

YOUNGSTOWN
STROUSS
20 W. Federal Street

MISSOURI

CLAYTON
WOODY'S
81 Plaza Frontenac

KANSAS CITY
WOOLF BROS.
1020 Walnut Street

ST. LOUIS
STIX, BAER & FULLER
Washington Avenue & 6th Street
FAMOUS-BARR
601 Olive Street

THE WEST

UTAH

SALT LAKE CITY
BARNEY'S
249 Trolley Square

COLORADO

BOULDER
LIVONI
1110 Spruce Street

COLORADO SPRINGS
PERKINS SHEARER
102 N. Tejon

DENVER
NEUSTETER'S
720 16th Street

OREGON

PORTLAND
LIPMAN'S
521 S.W. Fifth Avenue

MARIO'S
1223 Lloyd Center
MEIER AND FRANK
621 S.W. 5th Avenue

WASHINGTON

SEATTLE
BUTCH BLUM
1408 Fifth Avenue
NELLY'S STALLION
1311 N.E. 45th Street
NORDSTROM
1501 Fifth Avenue

THE COAST/CALIFORNIA

SAN FRANCISCO
JOSEPH MAGNIN
59 Harrison Street
I. MAGNIN
Union Square
L'UOMO
4141 18th Street
MACY'S
California, Stockton & O'Farrell Streets
ROOS-ATKINS
799 Market Street
THE FIRST CHANGE UP
3613 Sacramento Street
WILKES-BASHFORD
336 Sutter Street

CUPERTINO
THE POLO STORE OF CUPERTINO
2138 Vallco Fashion Park

PALO ALTO
THE POLO STORE
Stanford Shopping Center

LOS ANGELES
BULLOCK'S/CENTURY CITY
10250 Santa Monica Boulevard
BULLOCK'S/WILSHIRE
3050 Wilshire Boulevard
MAXFIELD BLEU
9091 Santa Monica Boulevard

ROBINSON'S
600 W. 7th Street

BEVERLY HILLS
ERIC ROSS
9636 Brighton Way
JERRY MAGNIN
323 N. Rodeo Drive
MR. GUY
369 N. Rodeo Drive

LA JOLLA
THE POLO STORE OF LA JOLLA
1030 Wall Street

INDEX

Note: page numbers in italics refer to illustrations